super duper soups

michael van straten

super duper soups

healing soups for the mind and body

mitchell beazley

Super Duper Soups
Michael van Straten

First published in Great Britain in 2008 by Mitchell Beazley,
an imprint of Octopus Publishing Group Limited,
2–4 Heron Quays, London E14 4JP.
An Hachette Livre UK Company
www.octopusbooks.co.uk

A CIP catalogue record for this book is available from the
British Library.

ISBN: 978 1 84533 332 4

While all reasonable care has been taken during the preparation
of this edition, neither the publisher, editors nor the author can
accept responsibility for any consequences arising from the use
thereof or from the information contained therein.

Super Duper Soups is meant to be used as a general recipe
book. While the author believes the recipes it contains are
beneficial to health, the book is in no way intended to replace
medical advice. You are urged to consult a physician about
specific medical complaints and the use of healing herbs and
foods in the treatment thereof.

Commissioning Editor: Rebecca Spry
Art Director: Tim Foster
Deputy Art Director: Yasia Williams-Leedham
Designer: Geoff Borin
Project Editor: Georgina Atsiaris
Editor: Jamie Ambrose
Proofreader: Sylvia Tombesi-Walton
Photographer: Simon Walton
Food stylist: Sue Henderson
Senior Production Controller: Lucy Carter
Indexer: Hilary Bird

Printed and bound by Toppan Printing Company in China
Typeset in Kievit

contents

introduction

'Beautiful soup, so rich and green,

Waiting in a hot tureen!

Who for such dainties would not stoop?

Soup of the evening, beautiful soup!

Beautiful soup! Who cares for fish,

Game, or any other dish?

Who would not give all else for two

Pennyworth only of beautiful soup?'

Lewis Carroll, from *Alice's Adventures in Wonderland*

There are so many wonderful quotes about soup that I could have filled the book with them, but this is one of my favourites. The fact that so many famous men and women of letters have written in such emotive terms about soup just illustrates what an important place it has in our hearts and mind – and, of course, on our kitchen and dining-room tables.

One of the truest quotations about soup comes, surprisingly, from the pen of Judith Martin. Known throughout America by her pen name, Miss Manners, she's renowned as a journalist, author and authority on etiquette. Her advice column is syndicated to hundreds of newspapers. In her book, *Miss Manner's Guide to Excruciatingly Correct Behaviour*, Miss Manners says:

'Do you have a kinder, more adaptable friend in the food world than soup? Who soothes you when you are ill? Who refuses to leave you when you are impoverished and stretches its resources to give a hearty sustenance and cheer? Who warms you in the winter and cools you in the summer?

Yet who also is capable of doing honor to your richest table and impressing your most demanding guests? Soup does its loyal best, no matter what undignified conditions are imposed upon it. You don't catch steak hanging around when you're poor and sick, do you?'

This is the essence of soup and the foundations on which the recipes in this book are built.

It's now more than five years since I wrote the first *Super Soups* book, never dreaming that my passion for those basic recipes with such healing properties for body, mind and soul would interest so many people. The book has sold worldwide, which is always exciting for an author, but for me, the most surprising event was seeing the translated French edition. After all, you couldn't imagine a better example of coals to Newcastle than an English soup book to France.

Since my wife, Sally, and I moved to France at the end of 2006 (a week before Christmas, would you believe), we've discovered just how important soups are as part of the French psyche, culture and lifestyle. We live in a delightful small town situated in the fruit garden of rural France, where the people are fiercely proud of the regional produce and cooking of Sarthe.

We're not far from the great *châteaux* of the Loire Valley, but most visitors are French, and there are only a few other British residents. Contrary to popular myth, the French really do like the Brits – as long as you're prepared to try to speak the language, join in community life and relish the local cooking. We do all three; consequently, we've made many French friends, from our elderly neighbours to the kids at the local school.

We find bags of home-grown produce hanging on the front door, jars of home-made preserves, bottled asparagus, jam and pâté on the doorstep – to say nothing of bottles of the very local Jasnières white wine presented to us as gifts.

Our culinary highlights have often been in small local bars and cafés, where for nine or ten euros you're served a four-course meal with wine. The food is the best of traditional peasant cooking, and some of the soups are extraordinary. As you'll find in this book, our local cooks are happy to divulge their secrets.

If you've already got the original *Super Soups*, you'll see that these recipes are very different, although the basic stocks and garnishes are much the same. Nothing is simpler than making a super soup. Most of these recipes are quick, they're all easy and generally incredibly good nutritional value for money.

They range from simple, hearty, peasant soups like Caldo Verde (*see* page 52), with onions, garlic, cabbage and smoked sausage and Beef 'n' Barley (*see* page 53), which is almost a stew, to lighter soups like My Thai (*see* page 28), with prawns, coriander and lemon grass or Spiced Lettuce Soup with Goat's Cheese (*see* page 69), and sophisticated, elegant recipes like Curried Fish and Herb (*see* page 86) with saffron and white fish and chilled fruit soups like Raspberry Relish (*see* page 18).

Here you'll find soups that warm, recipes that boost your immunity, care for your skin, improve your circulation and restore you to good health. There are also good-mood, slimming and sexy soups.

Home-made soup has to be the best food and health bargain in the world. You get bowlfuls of protein and the healthiest, low-glycaemic-index complex carbohydrates. You get protective vitamins, essential minerals, enzymes and all the amazing phytochemicals that help protect your body against heart disease, high blood pressure, circulatory problems and many types of cancer.

Once you start to make soup, you'll also make two great discoveries. Firstly, no matter how many times you make the same recipe, it always tastes different (unlike those tins you choose to buy from Messrs Campbell or Heinz). Secondly, soup is social superglue: sitting round a table with a bowl of soup binds friends and family together – which is precisely why, unless otherwise stated, each recipe in this book is designed to serve four people.

immunity-boosting soups

Thankfully, the body has its own natural defence mechanism that protects it against infectious organisms and from the internal damage that can be created by free radicals. This immune system depends on an adequate consumption of essential vitamins and minerals, enough natural protective plant chemicals and a generous supply of antioxidants to neutralize dangerous free radicals. There's no doubt that basic cleanliness and hygiene play a key role in defence, but if you allow your immune system to drop below its optimum efficiency, you're asking for trouble.

As well as all the essential nutrients, your body needs to be protected against 'anti-nutrients'. A high intake of bad fats, refined sugars and cereals, alcohol, junk food, smoking, and exposure to heavy metals such as cadmium, lead and mercury – not forgetting atmospheric pollution – can all compromise your natural immunity.

Modern intensive farming and horticulture don't help, either. Due to intensive rearing, artificial fertilizers, insecticides, pesticides and fungicides, a lot of commercially available foods may not only be contaminated with residues, but recent studies indicate that they are also likely to have lower levels of certain nutrients than good organic produce. Changing the way you eat so that you increase your consumption of immunity-boosting nutrients will almost certainly improve the effectiveness of your immune system. One of the least recognized causes of poor immunity is a lack of zinc, a mineral that is missing from many people's daily diets. Boost your intake by sprinkling toasted pumpkin or other seeds onto the soups, or by adding a few prawns, mussels or other shellfish where appropriate.

You can start improving your immune system by trying the recipes in this chapter. Good protein in the recipe for Turkey Twizzle (*see* page 16), for instance, is combined with betacarotene from the carrots, lycopene from the tomatoes and the protective phytochemicals in the onions, thyme and harissa paste to make this one-pot meal a real resistance booster. For a delicious immunity-boosting treat, try Raspberry Relish (*see* page 18). Resistance Soup (opposite) contains vitamin E from the almonds, anti-cancer chemicals from the broccoli and all the antibacterial, antiviral and antifungal protection from the garlic and onions.

Simple though they seem, these super soups really can boost your natural resistance.

Broccoli is a very rich source of carotenoids, especially betacarotene. This group of chemicals is known to restrict the development and growth of cancer cells. In Japan, for example, they have very little bowel cancer and they eat lots of all the cabbage family. In the UK, we get about a quarter of the protective chemicals of the cabbage family and have a very high incidence of bowel cancer.

resistance soup

Those of you who are old enough may remember the huge amount of attention all over the world when US president Ronald Reagan was found to have polyps in his colon. He was told they sometimes become cancerous and was advised to eat lots of broccoli. For years, naturopaths like me had been talking about the amazing immunity-boosting power of all members of the cabbage family, particularly their ability to help reduce bowel cancer.

onion 1 medium, finely chopped

garlic 2 cloves, smashed and finely chopped

rapeseed oil 2 tablespoons

broccoli 110g or 4oz, florets

vegetable stock 1.2 litres or 40fl oz – *see* page 104 or use a good stock cube or bouillon powder

almonds 75g or 3oz, slivered

pepper sauce 1 teaspoon

lemon juice from 1 lemon

1 In a large saucepan, gently sauté the onion and garlic in the oil until softened.

2 Add the broccoli and stock.

3 Simmer until the broccoli is just tender.

4 Put into a food processor or blender with the almonds and whiz until smooth.

5 Put back into the saucepan and add the pepper sauce and lemon juice to taste, then serve.

There are lots of anti-cancer and immunity-boosting **phytochemicals** in watercress. **Antibacterial** properties are found in garlic, and there are wonderful chest- and heart-protective effects from the onion.

cress and chorizo

The first hospital in the world was built by Hippocrates, who chose a site by a stream flowing with pure spring water just so that he could grow watercress for his patients. In 460BC, this Greek father of modern medicine had already described the protective and immunity-boosting properties of watercress. Combined with garlic and the chilli in the sausage, this is an instantly comforting and strengthening soup.

butter 10g or ¼oz, unsalted

chorizo sausage 150g or 5½oz, finely sliced

onion 1, finely sliced

garlic 1 large clove, smashed and finely sliced

flour 1 heaped tablespoon

vegetable stock 1 litre or 34fl oz – *see* page 104 or use a good stock cube or bouillon powder

watercress 1 large bunch, thick stems removed

crème fraîche about 350ml or 12fl oz

1 Melt the butter in a large saucepan and gently fry the sausage until crisp – about 10 minutes. Remove and set aside.

2 Add the onion and garlic and gently sauté, stirring continuously, until soft and golden.

3 Sprinkle on the flour, stir well and cook for another 2 minutes, again stirring continuously.

4 Pour in the stock and bring to a boil.

5 Tip in the watercress and crème fraîche, stir well and simmer for 2 minutes.

6 Whiz in a food processor or blender – or use a hand blender – until smooth.

7 Tip in the sausage, stir and leave off the heat for 2 minutes before serving.

vital statistics

As well as containing huge amounts of **vitamin C** and antioxidant **anthocyanosides**, currants are also a rich source of **potassium**, which helps protect against high blood pressure. The soluble fibre **pectin** in the apples helps lower cholesterol and also helps relieve the pain of rheumatism, arthritis and gout.

chill-out treat

An apple a day may keep the doctor away, but the two apples in this recipe, combined with the apple juice, make a powerful health-boosting combination. When you add the redcurrants, you get a fantastic boost of protective phytochemicals and vitamins, which not only increases your resistance to infectious bugs, but also gives your system a real shot in the arm of antioxidant heart-protective and cancer-fighting substances.

butter 10g or ¼oz, unsalted
runny honey 3 tablespoons
apples 2, quartered
redcurrants 400g or 14oz
apple juice 500ml or 17fl oz, organic

1 Melt the butter in a large saucepan and gently mix in the honey.

2 Add the apple quarters and stir until caramelized.

3 Reserving 4 small stems, tip in the redcurrants and apple juice. Continue cooking gently until the liquid is slightly reduced.

4 Put the mixture into a food processor or blender – or use a hand blender – and whiz until smooth.

5 Leave to chill thoroughly in the fridge.

6 Serve with the reserved redcurrants floating on top.

All the potatoes in this recipe provide a minuscule 200 calories – and that's split among four people. But they also give you immunity-boosting **vitamins B** and **C**. It's the mushrooms that are the real news here. Used as medicine for around 7,000 years, the shiitake mushroom is a specific immunity booster.

mushroom immunity

Let's set the record straight once and for all: good food means pleasure. Sadly, self-styled 'experts' make up for their lack of real knowledge by inventing diets of sackcloth and ashes. To these people, potatoes are poison, cream is death on your plate and butter is forbidden – what a load of rubbish! These foods make delicious dishes that act as suppliers of wonderful nutrients. Just try this fabulous soup and judge for yourself.

vegetable stock 1.2 litres or 40fl oz – *see* page 104 or use a good stock cube or bouillon powder

potatoes 225g or 8oz, peeled and diced

shiitake mushrooms 110g or 4oz, finely chopped

marjoram half a teaspoon, dried

onion 1 small, finely chopped

butter 50g or 2oz, unsalted

flour 1 heaped tablespoon

single cream 150ml or 5fl oz

1 Bring the stock to a boil in a large saucepan.

2 Add the potatoes, mushrooms and marjoram.

3 Adjust the heat to a simmer and cook until the potatoes are tender – about 30 minutes.

4 In another large saucepan, gently sauté the onion in the butter.

5 Sprinkle on the flour, stir until well combined and continue cooking for 2 minutes.

6 Add the soup to the onions one ladleful at a time (to avoid lumps), stirring constantly, then simmer, stirring until slightly thickened.

7 Whiz in a food processor or blender – or use a hand blender – until smooth.

8 Return to the pan, stir in the cream and reheat.

vital statistics

Protein, iron and B vitamins from the turkey, and a cocktail of carotenoids from the carrots, tomatoes and spinach are combined with the immunity-boosting essential oils in the bay, thyme, basil and harissa.

turkey twizzle

This looks like a long list of ingredients, but they're all very simple and more than worthwhile. Quite apart from its enormous immunity-boosting properties, this is a fabulous soup; just add some good wholemeal bread, a green salad and a glass of wine, and you've got a one-pot meal fit for a king (or queen). Lots of veg and protein, virtually no saturated fat, healing herbs and energy-packed carbohydrates – what more could you want?

olive oil 2 tablespoons

celery 2 stalks, finely diced

carrots 2, trimmed and peeled if not organic (organics just need to be scrubbed), finely diced

onion 1 medium, finely chopped

tomatoes 1 x 400g can, crushed

spinach 250g or 9oz, frozen

turkey 275g or 10oz, cooked and cubed

chicken stock 1.2 litres or 40fl oz – *see* page 106 or use a good stock cube or bouillon powder

bay leaves 2

thyme 1 large sprig

harissa paste 1 tablespoon

basil leaves 1 small handful, chopped

rice 110g or 4oz, cooked

1 Heat the olive oil in a large saucepan. Add the celery, carrots and onion and sauté gently until the vegetables are soft.

2 Add the crushed tomatoes.

3 Add the spinach, turkey, stock, bay leaves, thyme and harissa paste.

4 Simmer until the vegetables are tender and the turkey is heated through – about 15 minutes.

5 Remove the bay leaves and thyme and stir in the basil and rice to serve.

The enzyme **allinase** in onion and its relatives triggers the release of healing compounds. These help boost natural resistance, attack invading organisms, help lower cholesterol, reduce blood pressure and prevent blood clots.

vegetable power

Every spoonful of this super-resistance soup is packed with protective power. The allium family of plants is among the most potent of immunity boosters, and in this recipe there's onion, garlic and leek: all with the specific ability to fight chest infections, fungal attacks and heart problems. Add the particular nutrients in root vegetables and highly concentrated tomato purée and you have a soup everyone will enjoy. A real treat for vegetarians.

olive oil 2 tablespoons

onion 1 large, very finely chopped

garlic 2 cloves, smashed and finely chopped

flour 1 tablespoon

potatoes 2 medium, cut into small dice

carrots 2, trimmed and peeled if not organic (organics just need to be scrubbed), cut into small dice

courgettes 250g or 9oz, cubed

leek 1 small, finely sliced

parsnip 1 small, cut into small dice

vegetable stock 1.5 litres or 51fl oz – *see* page 104 or use a good stock cube or bouillon powder

tomato purée 4 tablespoons

1 Heat the oil in a large saucepan and gently sauté the onion. After a couple of minutes, add the garlic and sauté until soft.

2 Sprinkle over the flour and mix well.

3 Add the vegetables, stock and tomato purée.

4 Bring to a boil and simmer until the vegetables are cooked.

vital statistics

You'll get **vitamin C** and a high level of protective **antioxidants** from the raspberries, hugely powerful antibacterial benefits from the manuka honey and bone-building **calcium** from the milk.

raspberry relish

Like all berries, raspberries are at the top of the league table of 'ORAC' foods: the oxygen radical absorbance capacity method of measuring antioxidants in food. These delicious super-antioxidant berries lose very little of their immunity-boosting value through freezing, making this a great year-round, taste-of-summer soup. All natural honey has healing properties, but manuka, from New Zealand, is uniquely powerful.

raspberries 400g or 14oz; frozen fruit will do, defrosted and drained

milk 200ml or 7fl oz

manuka honey 2 tablespoons

single cream 150ml or 5fl oz

amaretti biscuits 6, crushed

1 Put the raspberries, milk, honey and cream into a food processor or blender and whiz until smooth.

2 Leave to chill thoroughly in the fridge.

3 Scatter the amaretti biscuits over to serve.

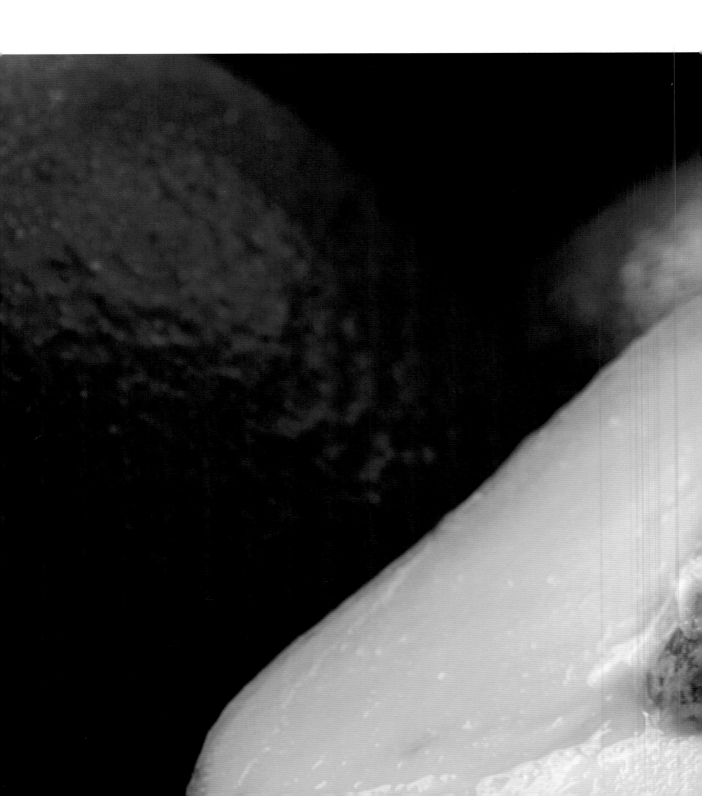

circulation soups

According to American food writer Mrs MFK Fisher, 'It is impossible to think of any good meal, no matter how plain or elegant, without soup or bread in it.' She died in 1992 at the age of 83, having written hundreds of stories for *The New Yorker*, the prestigious US magazine, as well as essays, many books and a great English translation of Brillat-Savarin's book, *The Physiology of Taste*. Fisher was always deeply concerned with the cultural importance of food, which I'm sure explains her love of soup.

It's impossible to ignore the enormous contribution made by nutrition to both the maintenance of a healthy heart and blood flow and the development of heart disease and blocked arteries. The former is thanks to healthy eating; the latter is due to excessive consumption of the wrong foods and not enough of the good. Since the beginning of the 20th century, naturopaths have known about these links and tried to teach their patients the importance of healthy eating.

Since the 1960s, naturopaths have been even more aware of the risks and benefits, and since the solving of the riddle of the 'French Paradox' in the 1980s, the general world of medicine has accepted that eating too much saturated fat is a major cause of raised cholesterol and narrowed arteries. With the dawn of the 21st century, the links between too much salt and high blood pressure became irrefutable. At the same time, it became increasingly obvious that eating more wholegrain cereals, legumes and oily fish had a strong and positive effect on cholesterol, blood pressure and heart disease.

I wrote about these things in the first *Super Soups* book, but it is only in the last 12 months that wholegrain cereals have been officially recognized as being good for the heart, and excessive salt consumption been seen as a direct cause of raised blood pressure, strokes and heart disease. As I write these words on 21 May 2007, NICE (National Institute for Clinic Excellence) has announced that all patients with heart disease should be prescribed fish oils.

Use the recipes in this chapter to protect yourself from circulatory problems and heart disease, but if it's too late and you already suffer from these conditions, it's doubly important to help your body to get rid of artery-clogging cholesterol with these therapeutic soups. Apple and Squash (*see* page 30), for example, has protective fibre. Hot Harissa (*see* page 25) is the spicy way to ginger up your circulation. Avocado, smoked salmon, okra, Tabasco sauce and tropical fruits in the other recipes all contain nutrients and phytochemicals that nourish, protect and heal your heart and blood vessels.

Smoked salmon is an excellent source of **omega-3** fatty acids. Avocados are equally rich in mono-unsaturated fatty acids. **Vitamin C** from the lemon juice helps to reduce the risk of blood clots. Tabasco, like the other chilli derivatives, stimulates blood flow.

avocado smokie

I'm no longer surprised by women who refuse to eat avocados in the false belief that they're unhealthy and fattening. Combined here with lemon juice, sour cream, Tabasco sauce and smoked salmon, they produce a soup that not only tastes great and would grace the most elegant dining table, but is also a cornucopia of health-giving and circulation-stimulating nutrients.

avocados 3 ripe, peeled, stones removed

lemon juice from 2 large lemons

sour cream about 300ml or 10fl oz

vegetable stock about 1.2 litres or 40fl oz – *see* page 104 or use a good stock cube or bouillon powder

Tabasco sauce 3 good dashes

smoked salmon 200g or 7oz best-quality

1 Put the avocado flesh into a food processor or blender with the lemon juice, sour cream, half the stock and the Tabasco, and whiz until smooth.

2 Add more of the stock to give you the texture you want.

3 Put into the fridge, covered, to chill for an hour – no longer, or it will discolour.

4 Chop the smoked salmon finely.

5 Stir half into the soup and serve the rest scattered on top.

vital statistics

You'll get a massive circulatory boost from the ginger, a blood-flow bonus from the hot harissa paste and lots of beneficial oils from the coriander. Lycopene, one of the most protective of all carotenoids, is more abundant in canned and puréed tomatoes than fresh.

hot harissa

For at least 5,000 years, herbs and spices have been used in food and as medicine to stimulate the circulation. Harissa is a prime example. Chillies, caraway, cumin, hot peppers and paprika are all used in this fabulous North African condiment. Ginger and fresh coriander leaves give an extra circulatory boost to this very different tomato soup. Be warned: one of the '57 varieties' it isn't!

butter 25g or 1 oz, unsalted

onion 1 medium, finely chopped

garlic 2 cloves, smashed and finely chopped

cumin 1 teaspoon, ground

ginger root 2.5cm or 1in fresh, grated

tomato purée 2 teaspoons

harissa 1 teaspoon

tomatoes 1 x 400g can, crushed

vegetable stock 1 litre or 34fl oz – see page 104 or use a good stock cube or bouillon powder

crème fraîche about 300ml or 10fl oz

coriander leaves 1 medium handful, finely chopped

1 Melt the butter in a large saucepan and gently sauté the onions and garlic until soft and golden.

2 Stir in the cumin and ginger and continue cooking for 2 more minutes, stirring well.

3 Add the tomato purée and harissa, stir well and continue cooking for 2 minutes.

4 Pour in the tomatoes and stock. Bring to a boil, then simmer for 20 minutes.

5 Tip the mixture into a food processor or blender – or use a hand blender – and whiz until smooth.

6 Whip the crème fraîche with the coriander leaves.

7 Serve the soup with the crème fraîche and coriander on top.

This soup supplies heart-friendly olive oil with **mono-unsaturated fat.** Garlic and onion contain protective chemicals. Courgettes provide **betacarotene.** Natural Greek yogurt delivers **calcium, protein** and friendly bacteria.

greek cold courgette soup

It's no coincidence that Greek men are the longest-lived in Europe and that Cretan men are the longest-lived in Greece. This is all down to their traditional diet, which is based on fish, olive oil, fruit, vegetables, nuts and seeds. On these foods, Greeks have the lowest level of heart and circulatory disease. This soup is a typical Cretan recipe, full of heart-friendly foods and containing nothing to interfere with good health.

olive oil 2 tablespoons

onion 1, finely chopped

garlic 1 clove, smashed and finely chopped

powdered ginger 1 level tablespoon

courgettes 2 large, cut into large cubes

lemon juice and zest of 1 large lemon

vegetable stock 1.2 litres or 40fl oz – *see* page 104 or use a good stock cube or bouillon powder

natural greek yogurt 4 tablespoons

1 Heat the oil in a large saucepan. Add the onion, garlic and ginger powder. Mix well and cook gently until the onion and garlic are soft – about 5 minutes.

2 Add the courgettes and lemon juice and zest and pour in the stock.

3 Bring to a boil and simmer gently until the courgettes are soft – about 20 minutes.

4 Whiz in a food processor or blender until smooth and return to the pan.

5 Add the yogurt, mix well and allow to cool.

6 Chill in the fridge until really cold.

vital statistics

Peanuts contain artery-protecting mono-unsaturated fats. Chilli, paprika and ginger are rich sources of plant chemicals that stimulate blood flow. Sweet potato has abundant supplies of skin- and immunity-protecting betacarotene.

sweet potato and peanut soup

Why on earth do so many people think peanuts are unhealthy? The truth is just the opposite: they help reduce cholesterol and prevent type-2 diabetes, both of which spell disaster for the circulation. The spices give your circulation a short, sharp boost and the rich supply of phytochemicals from the tomatoes and sweet potato all add to the heart and circulatory benefits of this African treasure.

peanut oil 2 tablespoons

onion 1 large, finely chopped

garlic 2 cloves, smashed and finely chopped

mushrooms 4 large, finely chopped

dried chilli flakes 1 teaspoon

paprika ½ teaspoon

ginger root 1cm or a ½in fresh, grated

vegetable stock 850ml or 29fl oz – *see* page 104 or use a good stock cube or bouillon powder

sweet potato 2 large, 1 peeled and cubed, 1 cooked and mashed

tomatoes 275g or 10oz, canned, with the juice

smooth peanut butter 4 heaped tablespoons

1 Heat the peanut oil in a large saucepan.

2 Add the onion, garlic and mushrooms and sauté gently until the onions are soft and golden.

3 Tip in the chilli flakes, paprika and ginger. Mix well and continue cooking gently for 2 more minutes.

4 Pour in the stock, tomatoes and cubed sweet potatoes and simmer until the potatoes are tender – about 15 minutes.

5 Whiz in a food processor or blender – or with a hand blender – until smooth.

6 Add the mashed sweet potato and the peanut butter and blend again.

7 Reheat, if necessary, to serve.

vital statistics

The ginger and chillies provide **phytochemicals**. **Protein** and **zinc** are abundant in the prawns, as are fat-free nutrients in the fish stock and mushrooms.

my thai

First it was Italian, then Indian, followed by Chinese; now all the ingredients for Thai cooking are in your local supermarket. As well as improving circulation, this is an all-round healthy soup that tastes fabulous and is very easy to make. Here again, ginger and chillies are the obvious ingredients to improve blood flow, but the absence of any animal fat makes this a double bonus for anyone with heart or circulatory problems.

fish stock 700ml or 24fl oz – *see* page 104 or use a good stock cube or bouillon powder

mushrooms 100g or 3½oz, finely chopped

lemon grass 1 small stick, very finely chopped

ginger root 2.5cm or 1 in fresh, peeled and finely grated

soy sauce 2 teaspoons

red chillies 3 small, deseeded and very finely chopped

coconut milk about 300ml or 10fl oz

prawns 4 large, cooked and peeled

coriander leaves 1 handful, chopped

1 Put the stock into a large saucepan and bring to a boil.

2 Add the mushrooms, lemon grass, ginger, soy sauce and chillies and boil for 5 minutes.

3 Add the coconut milk and prawns and leave to rest off the heat for 5 minutes.

4 Serve with the coriander sprinkled on top.

vital statistics

Pectin, the natural fibre in apples, helps reduce cholesterol. Pumpkins provide betacarotene for good skin and a strong immune system. Onions contain circulation- boosting phytochemicals.

apple and squash

If an apple a day keeps the doctor away, a bowl of this soup should keep you out of the clutches of medicine for a month. Spoon by spoon, you'll boost your immunity to all sorts of infections and help your body get rid of artery-clogging cholesterol. With heart- and circulation-protecting nutrients, this is a very simple and quick health-giving soup.

butter 25g or 1oz, unsalted

onion 1 medium, finely sliced

acorn squash 1 medium, peeled and cubed

apple juice 350ml or 12fl oz, organic

vegetable stock 350ml or 12fl oz – *see* page 104 or use a good stock cube or bouillon powder

apple 1 granny smith, cored (but not peeled) and diced

crème fraîche about 300ml or 10fl oz

1 Melt the butter in a large saucepan and sauté the onion and squash gently until the onion is golden – about 5 minutes.

2 Pour in the apple juice and stock, bring to a simmer and add the apple pieces.

3 Continue simmering until the vegetables are tender.

4 Whiz in a food processor or blender – or with a hand blender – until smooth.

5 Serve with a spoonful of crème fraîche in each bowl.

vital statistics

Pawpaws are a rich source of fibre, betacarotene, vitamins and minerals. Coriander, a spicy heart helper, also relieves aches and pains. Coconut milk does contain saturated fat, but it's a good source of iron and fibre with a unique taste – so don't overdo it.

pawpaw soup

Like most tropical fruits, pawpaws are both wonderfully tasty and incredibly healthy. They're a rich source of protective antioxidants, minerals and vitamins that help promote a healthy heart and circulation. They also contain a digestive enzyme called papain. Eaten on their own, pawpaws are a powerful prescription for a healthy heart and circulation. The coriander gives an added dimension since it's not only a traditional anti-inflammatory remedy in India, but has recently been shown to have cholesterol-lowering benefits, too.

pawpaws 3 large, ripe, peeled, pips removed and cut into small chunks

coconut milk 250ml or 9fl oz

milk 250ml or 9fl oz, semi-skimmed

runny honey 4 tablespoons

ground coriander 1 teaspoon

1 Put the pawpaw flesh into a large saucepan, add the coconut milk and milk and cook gently for 20 minutes.

2 Add the honey and whiz in a food processor or blender – or use a hand blender – until smooth.

3 Serve warm with the ground coriander sprinkled on top.

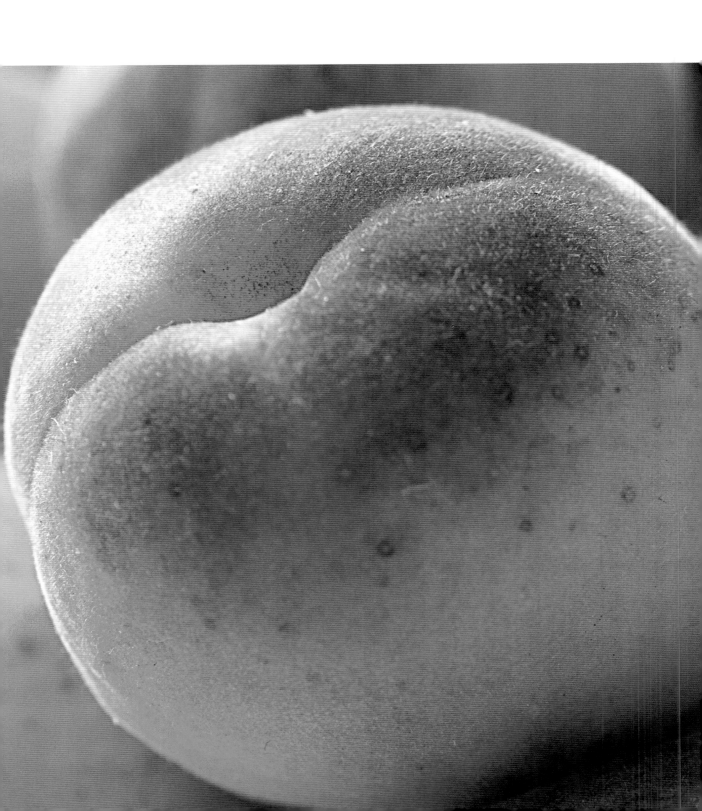

skin-reviving soups

In the endless search for eternal youth and beauty, women (and, increasingly, men) seem prepared to go to almost any lengths: plastic surgery, with all its risks of infection, rejection and anaesthetics; Botox injections, as likely to be administered by an unqualified beautician or money-grabbing GP as by a qualified plastic surgeon; painful skin peeling and a hundred other questionable therapies. Some people spend fortunes on dubious lotions, potions and treatments and as much again on miracle pills promoted by the latest charlatans whose celebrity connections get them on the TV or in the women's pages of national newspapers and magazines. Why bother, when the very first step should be a close look at your diet and lifestyle? A bottle of booze and 40 fags a day, combined with a lunatic low-calorie diet and meal replacements to stay thin, are going to make anyone, male or female, look 20 years older no matter what they spend on external treatments. A bad-hair day, a spotty-skin day, or a broken-nail day will be linked to nutritional excesses or deficiencies more often than you think.

Of course, not every skin problem is directly linked to food, but whatever the cause, better eating will mean improved skin and appearance, yet few dermatologists seem to think nutrition has any part to play in the treatment of skin conditions. Acne is a prime example in which medical opinion is absolutely against any dietary changes – they claim it will make no difference. After all my years in practice, I believe the opposite is true: although acne is triggered by hormone changes, improving the diet reduces the number of spots, calms the inflammation and helps lessen the amount of scarring. This is where Zit Zapper (*see* page 38) is a real bonus: it not only improves the skin, but also encourages youngsters to enjoy eating more skin-friendly vegetables.

Omega-3 fatty acids are powerful anti-inflammatories and have an important role in the relief of contact dermatitis and eczema. Soups such as Green and Pink (*see* page 39) provide these fats, plus lots of betacarotene and vitamin E, which are also important for healing the lesions and irritations of eczema. Strawberries, pumpkins, almonds, apricots, carrots, spinach and broccoli are all providers of essential skin nutrients. Onions, garlic, leeks and herbs and spices such as rosemary, chervil, cinnamon and star anise contain a range of phytochemicals that are cleansing, antiseptic and antibacterial. Whether it's winter warmth you are after or a refreshing chilled soup in summer, all these recipes are as delicious as they are healthy and good for your skin.

vital statistics

Selenium, vitamins A, B_1, B_2, B_3, B_6, folic acid, C, E and K are all found in spinach. Goat's cheese provides cell-building **protein** and **calcium**. There's more calcium and, importantly, **riboflavin** (B_2) in the cream.

spinach spot stopper

Popeye was wrong about spinach: it's not much good as a source of iron and strength. There's lots of iron in the leaves, but you can't get much out during digestion. However, spinach does contains very large amounts of betacarotene, which is one of the key nutrients for blemish-free, beautiful skin. A 175g or 6oz portion of spinach has only around 40 calories, but contains 10 days' worth of vitamin K, three days' worth of vitamin A and almost a day's worth of folic acid and manganese.

rapeseed oil 2 tablespoons

spinach 1kg or 2lb 4oz young leaves, roughly chopped

chervil half a handful, fresh

double cream 250ml or 9fl oz

goat's cheese about 200g or 7oz, soft

1 Heat the oil in a large saucepan.

2 Add the spinach and 700ml or 24fl oz water. Bring to a boil, then reduce to a simmer and cook until the spinach is wilted – about 5 minutes. Don't drain.

3 Add the chervil and whiz in a food processor – or use a hand blender – until smooth. Return to the pan.

4 Pour in half the cream and stir well.

5 Lightly whisk the rest of the cream, then mix well with the goat's cheese.

6 Pour the soup into serving bowls and serve with a dollop of the goat's cheese mixture on top.

vital statistics

This soup provides masses of **betacarotene** and **fibre** in the pumpkin, **vitamin A** and **calcium** in the Parmesan and natural sugars and **vitamin C** from the grapes.

two p's in a pod

For 40 years, I've argued with dermatologists about the vital link between food and skin. Nutrition is always at the bottom of their agenda, but the right food is essential to maintain healthy skin and to help improve many skin problems. Two key nutrients for good skin are vitamin A and betacarotene, which is now known to have a vital role of its own, as well as being a nutrient that the body converts to vitamin A. Pumpkin, like all yellow, orange and red produce, is a particularly rich source. Enjoy this smooth and velvety soup, which is as good for the soul as it is for the skin.

pumpkin or squash flesh, 1kg or 2lb 4oz, cubed

butter 25g or 1oz, unsalted

flour 1 tablespoon

crème fraîche 300ml or 10fl oz

ground coriander ½ teaspoon

parmesan cheese 150g or 5½oz, grated

grapes 1 large handful, seedless and thin-skinned

1 Put the pumpkin or squash in a large saucepan. Cover with water, bring to a boil and simmer for 10 minutes. Drain, reserving the cooking water.

2 Put the butter in a large saucepan, sprinkle in the flour and cook gently, stirring continuously, for 2 minutes until well combined.

3 Slowly add 1 litre or 34fl oz of the cooking water, stirring continuously.

4 Add the squash or pumpkin flesh and simmer for 10 minutes.

5 Mix in the crème fraîche, ground coriander, Parmesan and half the grapes.

6 Whiz until smooth in a food processor or blender – or use a hand blender.

7 Put back into the saucepan and reheat.

8 Serve with the rest of the grapes floating on top.

vital statistics

You'll get unique and powerful antioxidant proteins and masses of betacarotene for healthy skin from sweet potatoes. Crab is rich in often-deficient selenium and zinc. Sweet potatoes also protect against heart, skin and lung disease through betacarotene and vitamin B$_6$.

zit zapper

It's often a struggle to persuade teenagers to eat healthily, but I've found in my practice that vanity can be the key to encouraging a better diet. Nothing turns the youngsters on to fruit and veg quicker than the thought of banishing zits. Sweet potatoes give this soup an extra-large portion of skin-healing nutrients. The shallots, garlic and chives all attack bacteria that cause infections. The crab meat, like all shellfish, is rich in minerals.

shallots 4, finely chopped

garlic 2 cloves, smashed and finely chopped

olive oil 3 tablespoons

sweet potatoes 4, peeled and finely diced

double cream 150ml or 5fl oz

milk 200ml or 7fl oz

flour 2 tablespoons

crab meat 275g or 10oz, flaked

chives half a handful, snipped

1 Gently sauté the shallots and garlic in the oil.

2 Add the sweet potatoes and 350ml or 12fl oz water.

3 Bring to a boil, then simmer until the potatoes are tender, adding a little more water if the vegetables seem to be drying out.

4 Mash the vegetables well in the water.

5 In a separate bowl, mix together the cream, milk and flour, stirring well.

6 Add to the soup, bring back to a simmer and continue cooking, stirring constantly, until it thickens.

7 Stir in the crab meat and continue simmering for 2 more minutes.

8 Serve with the chives scattered on top.

Vitamin E and mono-unsaturated fats in the olive oil help reduce cholesterol and promote a healthy heart. Broccoli is a super-rich source of betacarotene and vitamins C and K and, like all its relatives, is also a super source of phytochemicals that help protect against the growth and spread of cancers.

green and pink

Olive oil, tuna and broccoli put this soup at the top of the class when it comes to caring for your skin. The combination of mono-unsaturated and omega-3 fats, betacarotene, vitamin C, minerals and protein provides a dermatological cocktail of unique efficacy. But that's not all: this particular complex package of nutrients is equally good for your heart, circulation and immune system. As a real bonus, it tastes fantastic, too.

olive oil 3 teaspoons

butter 25g or 1oz, unsalted

broccoli 3 large heads, (the stems can be used for making vegetable stock – *see* page 104)

vegetable stock 1 litre or 34fl oz – *see* page 104 or use a good stock cube or bouillon powder

tuna about 150g or 5oz (drained weight) canned in olive oil

four-spice powder 1 tablespoon

crème fraîche 200ml or 7fl oz

1 Heat the oil and butter in a large saucepan and tip in the broccoli heads.

2 Stir them around gently for 5 minutes, then add the stock.

3 Bring to a boil and simmer for 20 minutes.

4 Leave to cool, then chill in the fridge for at least 2 hours.

5 Meanwhile, drain the tuna, mix with the spices and flake gently to break up the fish.

6 Just before serving, stir the crème fraîche into the soup and mix well without breaking up the broccoli florets.

7 Serve the soup with the spiced tuna floating on top.

Rhubarb, an underrated medicinal plant, has been valued as a cleanser since the Middle Ages. Strawberries, very rich in **vitamin C** and with some well-absorbed **iron**, are also rich in **antioxidants** that can help delay the effects of ageing.

face-mask special

Helena Rubinstein famously said that women shouldn't put anything on their faces that they wouldn't put into their mouths. This unusual cold soup is a perfect example, bursting with vitamin C and healing phytochemicals from the fruit, essential oils from the spices and a gentle boost to the circulation from the small amount of alcohol. You probably could put it on your skin, but it will do more good and give you much more pleasure if you eat it.

rhubarb 450g or 1lb, sliced

strawberries 225g or 8oz, washed and hulled, plus a few for garnish

orange juice 450ml or 16fl oz

cinnamon 5cm or 2in stick

star anise 2 pods (optional)

caster sugar 50g or 2oz

grand marnier 3 tablespoons (optional)

mascarpone 4 tablespoons

1 Put the rhubarb, strawberries, orange juice, cinnamon stick and star anise into a large saucepan.

2 Bring to a boil and cook until the rhubarb is tender (about 10 to 15 minutes).

3 Take out the cinnamon stick and star anise.

4 Add the sugar and stir until it dissolves.

5 Whiz in a food processor or blender until smooth, strain into a large bowl and stir in the Grand Marnier.

6 Put into the fridge until really cold.

7 Serve with a dollop of mascarpone in each bowl and scatter with a few strawberry pieces.

warming soups

As a small boy I was often in trouble at school. On one occasion, my punishment was being kept in for a whole weekend and made to learn Gray's 'Elegy Written in a Country Churchyard', a poem that has stuck in my mind for more years than I care to remember. At that age I needed all sorts of tricks to create mental pictures so that I wouldn't forget the vital words when I had to stand up and recite the poem on Monday morning.

To help with the first verse, I always pictured the ploughman plodding his way home to a warming bowl of one of my mother's wonderful soups. Many of her recipes, like Ploughman's Soup (opposite), had their roots firmly embedded in the peasant traditions of Russia, the original home of my mother's family. The other influences on her cooking came from her Dutch mother-in-law, my paternal grandmother. The rigours of winter in Siberia and the icy winds blowing off the North Sea across the bleak, flat fields of Holland made warming soups essential for survival, as well as comfort and pleasure. Broad Bean and Chickpea Soup (see page 48) is an inexpensive but nourishing recipe, thanks to the protein in the beans and chickpeas and the warming calories from the potatoes. Few peasants could afford large quantities of meat, and this soup is a great substitute.

Even in the sunnier climes of Spain and Portugal, warming soups are great favourites and widely enjoyed. If your only memory of cabbage soup comes from the eponymous diet, now's the time to think again. Caldo Verde (see page 52) has the most wonderful flavour, plus all the nutrients you need to sustain you on a cold winter's day. All the soups in this chapter are not only warming, but also highly nutritious. Although you can enjoy any one of them at any time, they do have the bonus of specific health benefits, too.

My great interest in food has grown even stronger since Sally and I moved to France. But even here, in the Mecca of food traditions, the 21st century has begun to intrude. I recently picked up a booklet in our local supermarket, the cover of which had four powerful instructions: refuse the spread of fast food; refuse the loss of seasons; refuse the impoverishment of flavour; refuse the globalization of taste. Among other recommendations to strike a chord with me was that the best tool to encourage children to eat well is education, and the best way to expand everyone's interest in food is to promote a culture of curiosity. You'll probably need all the curiosity you can muster to try Hot, Sweet and Spicy Soup (see page 49), since the mixture of egg yolk, curry, chilli and cocoa does sound a bit strange. But it tastes great, and when I first had it in a torrential rainstorm in Brazil, it was certainly warming.

vital statistics

This is a strengthening soup, with bone-building calcium from the cheese, essential B vitamins from the beer, protective nutrients from the vegetables and plenty of warming calories.

ploughman's soup

The curfew tolls the knell of parting day,

The lowing herd wind slowly o'er the lea,

The ploughman homeward plods his weary way,

And leaves the world to darkness and to me.

When Thomas Gray wrote his 'Elegy Written in a Country Churchyard' in the middle of the 18th century, I'm certain that his weary ploughman was plodding home to a bowl of warming soup just like this. His wife would have used lard instead of rapeseed oil, the beer was probably home-brewed and Coleman's mustard didn't appear for another 50 years or so. But ground dried mustard was produced in England in 1720 and the warming flavours haven't changed with time.

rapeseed oil 2 tablespoons

celery 2 stalks, very finely diced

carrot 1 large, trimmed and peeled if not organic (organics just need to be scrubbed), finely cubed

onion 1, finely chopped

flour 1 tablespoon

dried mustard 1 teaspoon

vegetable stock 600ml or 20fl oz – *see* page 104 or use a good stock cube or bouillon powder

ale or strong beer (like Guinness), 300ml or 10fl oz

cheddar 175g or 6oz

1 Heat the oil in a large saucepan and sauté the vegetables gently until soft and golden.

2 Mix together the flour and mustard. Sprinkle over the vegetables, mix well and cook gently for 2 minutes.

3 Pour in the stock and ale, bring to a boil, then reduce to a simmer.

4 Tip in the cheese, stir well and continue simmering, stirring well, for 20 minutes.

vital statistics

Lentils provide **energy**, **fibre**, **folic acid** and iron. Feel-good essential oils come from thyme and bay leaves, while onions and garlic offer winter protection.

lovely lentils

This soup is the embodiment of that wonderful image we all have of a great pot of warming peasant soup bubbling on the stove. Yes, there is bacon, which means salt and fat, but it's a very small percentage of the total and there's no other animal fat in the recipe. Lentils may be small, but nutritionally they're mightily powerful. Some studies have indicated that a diet rich in legumes such as lentils can significantly reduce your risk of dying from heart disease. This is a comforting soup, with slow-release energy that also controls blood sugar and helps get rid of bad cholesterol.

olive oil 3 tablespoons

bacon 110g or 4oz, cut into thin strips crosswise – or the same amount of tofu, cubed

onions 2 small, finely chopped

celery 2 stalks, sliced

garlic 6 cloves, minced

puy lentils 175g or 6oz

tomatoes 1 x 400g can, crushed

vegetable stock 600ml or 20fl oz – *see* page 104 or use a good stock cube or bouillon powder

thyme 3 sprigs

bay leaves 2

1 Heat the oil in a large saucepan.

2 Add the bacon, onions and celery and cook until soft – about 10 minutes.

3 Add the garlic and stir for about 1 minute until soft.

4 Add the lentils and stir until coated with the oil and fat.

5 Add the tomatoes, stock, thyme and bay leaves, bring to a boil and simmer for about 35 minutes, or until the lentils are cooked.

6 Remove the thyme and bay leaves before serving.

vital statistics

Very low in fat, this soup provides healthy warming calories. The canned tomatoes add cancer-protective lycopene. Oregano provides antibacterial essential oils.

broad bean and chickpea soup

A bowl of steaming, warming, thick soup: exactly what you'll get from this recipe. But this isn't just empty calories; the special fibre in the beans and chickpeas protects the heart and circulation by lowering cholesterol, and the garlic and onion are perfect winter protectors. And, of course, the cayenne pepper adds a bit more heat to the bowl.

rapeseed oil 2 tablespoons

onion 1 medium, very finely chopped

garlic 1 clove, smashed and finely chopped

tomatoes 275g or 10oz, canned, chopped

ground coriander 1 teaspoon

cayenne pepper 2 pinches

vegetables stock 1.2 litres or 40fl oz – *see* page 104 or use a good stock cube or bouillon powder

potatoes 2 large, peeled and finely diced

chickpeas 275g or 10oz, canned, drained

broad beans 175g or 6oz, fresh or frozen

oregano leaves 1 small handful fresh (or 3 teaspoons dried), finely chopped

1 Heat the oil in a large saucepan and gently sauté the onions and garlic until soft and golden.

2 Tip in the tomatoes, coriander and cayenne pepper and simmer for 10 minutes.

3 Pour in the stock, potatoes, chickpeas and broad beans and continue simmering until the chickpeas and beans are tender – about 30 minutes.

4 About 5 minutes before serving, sprinkle on the oregano.

vital statistics

Cooking the rice in good stock means it absorbs all the nutrients from the vegetables. The stimulating oils from the chillies boost the circulation, and the spicy curry powder adds more tropical heat to this strange but delicious soup.

hot, sweet and spicy soup

Egg yolk, curry, cocoa and chilli in the same soup sounds disgusting. Thankfully, I had no idea of the ingredients when I first tasted this. I'd been travelling for three days: London, Frankfurt, Rio de Janeiro, São Paulo and finally Manaus, the capital of Amazonas, Brazil. I ate this soup in a street-side café a stone's throw away from the Rio Negro: little more than a tin shack with a sheet of sacking between the diners and the kitchen. It was a meeting place of South American cultures: the rainforest Indians, the Spanish, the Portuguese and, of course, the French. Raw eggs are not suitable for young children and the elderly.

butter 25g or 1oz, unsalted

onion 1, finely chopped

chillies 2, deseeded and very finely chopped

rice 60g or 2¼oz, long-grain

vegetable stock 1 litre or 34fl oz – *see* page 104 or use a good stock cube or bouillon powder

crème fraîche 200ml or 7fl oz

cocoa powder 1 tablespoon

curry powder 1 tablespoon

egg yolk 1

1 Heat half the butter in a large frying pan and sauté the onion and chillies until golden. Set aside.

2 In a large saucepan, cook the rice in the stock according to the packet instructions – normally about 10 minutes.

3 Add the onions and chillies and whiz the mixture in a food processor or blender – or use a hand blender.

4 Soften the rest of the butter slightly and mix with the crème fraîche, cocoa powder, curry powder and the egg yolk.

5 Add to the rice mixture and mix well.

vital statistics

Protein, B vitamins and iron are present in abundance in the lamb, while the vegetables provide fibre and minerals. Cumin adds digestive benefits, anti-cancer properties and Middle Eastern flavour.

shepherds' watch

In 1949 Louis DeGouy, chef at the Waldorf Astoria in New York for 30 years, wrote in *The Soup Book*: 'It breathes reassurance, it offers consolation; after a weary day it promotes sociability. There is nothing like a bowl of hot soup, its wisp of aromatic steam teasing the nostrils into quivering anticipation.' How true of this comforting, nourishing and sustaining dish. But is it a soup or a stew? I don't think it matters.

lamb 350g or 12oz fillet, cut finely along the grain into 1cm or ½in dice

onion 1, very finely chopped

cumin 1 teaspoon

rapeseed oil 2 tablespoons

tomato purée 1 tablespoon

lamb stock 1.5 litres or 51fl oz – *see* page 105 or use a good stock cube or bouillon powder

turnip 1 medium, peeled and diced

celery 3 stalks, sliced

potato 1 large, peeled and diced

1 Put the lamb, onions and cumin into a frying pan with the oil and cook, stirring continuously, until the lamb is just pink – about 5 minutes (or longer if you prefer your meat well done).

2 Add the tomato purée and stir well. Set aside.

3 Pour the stock into a large saucepan, tip in the turnips, celery and potatoes, bring to a boil and simmer until the vegetables are cooked – about 15 minutes.

4 Smash the vegetables roughly with a potato masher.

5 Add the lamb mixture and heat through gently.

vital statistics

What could be more basic than a soup made of sausage, cabbage and potatoes? But as well as being warming, it's nutritionally extremely valuable, providing cancer, heart and circulatory protection from the cabbage, onion and garlic. There are lots of minerals from the vegetable stock, with protein and iron in the sausage. Yes, there will be some saturated fat from the chorizo, but there's less than 25g or 1oz per portion.

caldo verde

Before moving to France, Sally and I were lucky to have the best neighbours in the world, Denzil and Verity. Together with their delightful daughters, Morgie and Meri, we shared many wonderful meals. Sally and Verity were always amused by their husbands, in their pinnies, swapping recipes over the garden fence. Denzil spent some years working in Spain, where this traditional Portuguese recipe was a favourite.

onion 1 large, finely sliced

garlic 2 cloves, smashed and finely chopped

rapeseed oil 3 tablespoons

chorizo sausage 110g or 4oz, cubed

vegetable stock 1.5 litres or 51fl oz – *see* page 104 or use a good stock cube or bouillon powder

cabbage 1 medium Savoy (the darker, the better), finely shredded

potatoes 4 large Desiree, peeled and finely diced

paprika 4 pinches

olive oil extra-virgin, for serving

1 Put the onion and garlic into a large saucepan.

2 Add the oil and soften over a low heat – about 5 minutes.

3 Add the chorizo and cook for a further 5 minutes.

4 Pour in the stock, add the cabbage and potatoes and simmer for 20 minutes until the potatoes are soft.

5 Serve sprinkled with the paprika and a drizzle of olive oil.

vital statistics

A perfect winter-protective combination, with **energy** and **fibre** from the barley, antibacterial **phytochemicals** from leeks and onions, and blood-strengthening **iron, B vitamins** and **protein** from the steak.

beef 'n' barley

Sadly, barley is often neglected in modern cooking, but it's a really healthy and beneficial grain. In fact, it's the oldest of all cultivated cereals and even the ancient Romans used it as a strength-giving food for their gladiators. Used in this soup with lean steak and cabbage, it's perfect in your vacuum flask for a cold winter day, or as a warming and sustaining meal when work is done.

pot barley 150g or 5½oz

leek 1, finely chopped

turnip 2 small (or 1 large), cubed

onion 1, finely chopped

beef stock 1.5 litres or 51fl oz – *see* page 105 or use a good stock cube or bouillon powder

braising steak 350g or 12oz, fat removed and finely cubed

cabbage half a small one, core removed and finely sliced

parsley 1 handful, finely chopped

1 Soak the barley in a generous amount of water, leave for an hour and drain.

2 Put the leek, turnip, onion, barley and stock in a large saucepan, bring to a boil and simmer for 45 minutes.

3 Add the meat and continue cooking for a further 30 minutes.

4 Tip in the cabbage and parsley and continue simmering for 10 minutes until the cabbage is cooked.

restorative soups

Convalescence used to be an integral part of all medical treatments. A period of time that allowed recovery from illness or operation was considered an essential part of the cure. Nutritional needs will depend on the type of illness, but the general principles include all the restorative foods. These need to be easily digestible, nutrient-rich, appetizing and easy-to-eat foods. The antioxidant vitamins A, C and E, protective minerals such as zinc, and a high intake of iron to ensure good haemoglobin are essential.

In her famous book *The Doctor in the Kitchen*, published in the 1930s, English writer Mrs Arthur Webb says: 'Food properly prepared and given to the invalid in the right quantities at the right time is of vital importance to build up strength and put the invalid on the road to health.' She insists on attractive presentation, a variety of crockery and scrupulous hygiene and provides recipes for beef teas, jellies, broths, fish, vegetables and restorative cordials.

Hospital diets are notoriously poor. They would strain the well-being of a healthy person, let alone someone recovering from serious illness or major surgery. A lack of fresh fruit, unappetizing salads and overcooked vegetables kept warm for hours result in severe depletion of vitamin C. This, in turn, makes the patient more liable to infection, promotes slower wound healing and can foster the development of bedsores.

A study by Professor John Garrow in 1994 indicates that poor quality hospital food can double the number of days spent in hospital by elderly patients recovering from fractures of the hip. Conversely, observations on well-nourished older patients demonstrate that giving them a simple vitamin and mineral supplement daily shortens the time it takes for them to recover from infectious illnesses.

Traditionally, all recipe books used to contain a section on invalid, convalescent and restorative cookery, and the soups in this chapter provide some of the best simple, appetizing and restorative recipes. These include Honey and Spice and All Things Nice (*see* page 64), with iron-rich chicory, protein and stimulating spices; Cold and Fizzy Kiwi (*see* page 65), with a huge amount of vitamin C and other strengthening nutrients; and Five-A-Day Soup (*see* page 60), which is overflowing with protective, repairing and restorative nutrients and antioxidants.

vital statistics

Cynarin in the artichoke hearts improves liver function, stimulates the gall bladder and encourages fat digestion and nutrient absorption. Milk and cheese are excellent sources of body-building **protein**, bone-strengthening **calcium** and high-energy calories. Sulphur-based chemicals in the onion help prevent infection.

hearty help

Frequently, even minor illnesses can lead to unpleasant and lingering digestive problems. More serious conditions involving the liver or gall bladder can make the digestion of fats a serious problem. If this happens, the body's absorption of the fat-soluble vitamins A, D, E and K is soon compromised, resulting in delayed recovery. The artichoke in this soup improves fat digestion, encouraging quicker recovery.

butter 50g or 2oz, unsalted

onion 1 medium, finely chopped

carrot 1 large, trimmed and peeled if not organic (organics just need to be scrubbed), grated

celery 2 sticks, finely diced

flour 2 tablespoons

vegetable stock 600ml or 20fl oz – *see* page 104 or use a good stock cube or bouillon powder.

milk 400ml or 14fl oz

cheddar cheese 225g or 8oz, grated

artichoke hearts 400g or 14oz (drained weight), rinsed and quartered

1 Put the butter into a large saucepan and sauté the onion, carrots and celery, stirring constantly, until tender.

2 Sprinkle in the flour, mix well and continue cooking for 2 more minutes.

3 Add the stock and milk, continue stirring and bring back to a simmer.

4 Tip in the cheese and stir until melted.

5 Add the artichoke hearts and continue simmering until warmed through – about 10 minutes.

vital statistics

This soup provides **bioflavonoids** to boost defences, **carotenoids** to protect the eyes, and antibacterial **essential oils** from the thyme.

pepper power

If you're just getting over a rotten cold, a bout of flu or a stay in hospital, this is the soup you need to restore your body and mind to tip-top performance. Sweet peppers are not only an enormous source of vitamin C – more than a day's dose from a mere 100g or 3½oz – they also supply considerable amounts of betacarotene, and this increases as they ripen from green to red. Protection against arthritis, heart and circulatory disease, some types of cancer and loss of vision all come from these simple and delicious fruits.

rapeseed oil 2 tablespoons

onion 1, finely chopped

paprika 2 teaspoons

flour 1 tablespoon

peppers 2 red, 1 yellow, deseeded and finely chopped

vegetable stock 1 litre or 34fl oz – *see* page 104 or use a good stock cube or bouillon powder

thyme 1 large sprig

mascarpone 225g or 8oz

black olives 75g or 3oz, stoned, roughly chopped

1 Heat the oil in a large saucepan. Add the onions and paprika, stir well and sauté gently until the onions are soft.

2 Sprinkle on the flour and mix in well.

3 Add the peppers, stock and thyme. Bring to the boil and simmer until the peppers are soft.

4 Whiz in a food processor or blender – or use a hand blender – until smooth and return to the pan.

5 Bring back to a simmer and gradually add the mascarpone, mixing well.

6 Serve with the olives scattered on top.

vital statistics

Lycopene in the tomatoes protects the eyes and the prostate. Protein and phytoestrogens from the beans rebuild tissues and help hormone problems. Natural cancer-fighting chemicals are abundant in the kale. Essential oils in the coriander stimulate appetite.

five-a-day soup

I'd normally run a mile from any recipe calling for 15 ingredients. But in addition to its restorative properties, this spicy soup tastes great and is easy to make. It's really worth the effort as it actually tastes better by the second or third day. It's a blockbuster restorative soup, with virtually every protective nutrient you can think of – and a lot more besides.

vegetable stock 1 litre or 34fl oz – *see* page 104 or use a good stock cube or bouillon powder

onion 1 medium, very finely chopped

garlic 3 cloves, finely chopped

pepper 1 medium green, finely diced

green chillies 6 small, sweet, deseeded and finely chopped

chilli powder 1 teaspoon

courgette 1 medium, diced

kale 2 handfuls, roughly torn

tomatoes 225g or 8oz, canned, crushed

kidney beans 225g or 8oz, canned, rinsed

sweetcorn 225g or 8oz, canned

oregano & cumin 1 teaspoon each, dried

sesame seeds 2 tablespoons, toasted

coriander 3 heaped tablespoons, fresh, chopped

1 Heat 1 tablespoon of stock in a large saucepan.

2 Add the onion, garlic, green pepper and green chillies and simmer, stirring constantly, for 5 minutes.

3 Add the chilli powder and continue cooking, again stirring constantly, for another minute.

4 Pour in the rest of the stock and add the courgettes, kale, tomatoes, beans, sweetcorn, oregano and cumin.

5 Bring to a boil, reduce the heat and simmer for 20 minutes.

6 Add the sesame seeds and fresh coriander just before serving.

Haddock offers high **protein**, low fat and lots of **minerals**. Split peas provide **B vitamins** and small amounts of **iron**, **zinc** and **calcium**. The fish stock supplies well-absorbed minerals and enzymes.

peas with fish

Fish of all sorts has long been a traditional food in sickroom cooking. For anyone convalescing, the easily digested protein, the absence of artery-clogging saturated fat and the rich spread of vitamins and minerals in the fish in this soup mean several steps up the ladder to recovery. The delicate flavour of smoked haddock gently tempts the taste buds, and the addition of split peas gives an extra energy and fibre boost.

rapeseed oil 2 tablespoons

onion 1, finely chopped

split peas 250g or 9oz, covered generously with water and soaked overnight

bouquet garni 1

fish or vegetable stock 1.2 litres or 40fl oz – *see* page 104 or use a good stock cube or bouillon powder

smoked haddock 400g or 14oz

1 Heat the oil in a large saucepan and sauté the onions gently until golden.

2 Add the split peas, bouquet garni and stock.

3 Bring to a boil and simmer until the peas are soft – about 30 minutes.

4 Remove the bouquet garni.

5 Whiz in a food processor or blender – or use a hand blender – until smooth and return to the pan.

6 Cut the fish into small cubes, add them to the soup and simmer gently until cooked through – about 5 minutes.

vital statistics

Special flavonoids **rutin** and **quercitin**, combined with **anethole**, make fennel an unusually generous provider of phytochemicals. Lots of **fibre**, **folic acid** and **potassium** – again in the fennel – add to the benefits.

fennel soup

American Dr James Duke is one of the world's leading ethno-botanists and an expert on the medicinal benefits of all plants. He is famously quoted as saying: 'An old-fashioned vegetable soup, without any enhancement, is a more powerful anti-carcinogen than any known medicine.' This is a great example. Eating can be a major problem when you're getting over any sort of illness, and this soup is a brilliant solution. The Greeks, Romans, Anglo-Saxons and the American Puritans all understood the value of fennel as both food and medicine. It stimulates the digestion and uniquely helps reduce inflammation and prevent some cancers. The gnocchi provide valuable energy for convalescence.

rapeseed oil 2 tablespoons

fennel 3 bulbs, finely sliced

onion 1, very finely chopped

garlic 2 cloves, smashed and very finely chopped

flour 2 tablespoons

vegetable stock 1 litre or 34fl oz – *see* page 104 or use a good stock cube or bouillon powder

crème fraîche 200ml or 7fl oz

gnocchi 110g or 4oz

1 Heat the oil in a large saucepan. Add the fennel, onion and garlic and sauté gently until golden – about 5 minutes.

2 Sprinkle on the flour and continue cooking for another 2 minutes.

3 Pour in the stock, bring to a boil, then reduce to a simmer.

4 Add the crème fraîche and stir well.

5 In another saucepan, cook the gnocchi following the packet instructions.

6 Serve the soup with the gnocchi floating on top.

vital statistics

Prebiotic **fibre** from the endive helps feed friendly bacteria. You'll get instant **energy** from the easily available gingerbread calories, plus stimulating spices.

honey and spice and all things nice

Rapeseed oil has the very best balance between omega-3 and -6 fatty acids and a high smoking point, which means you can cook at much higher temperatures. This results in faster cooking, less oil being absorbed by the food and much less risk of the dangerous by-products of overheated fats and oils. Two heads of chicory (endive or witloof) provide a scant 17 calories, a quarter of your daily fibre needs, lots of potassium and only 5mg of salt; consequently, this is a valuable restorative vegetable. With lots of protein and delicious calories from the gingerbread, this soup will stimulate the most jaded appetite.

rapeseed oil 2 tablespoons

butter 10g or ¼oz, unsalted

ham 150g or 5½oz, smoked, cut into small cubes

chicory 4 heads, roughly chopped

milk 600ml or 20fl oz, full-fat

gingerbread 200g or 7oz, cubed

crème fraîche 300ml or 10fl oz

1 Put the oil and butter into a large frying pan and sauté the smoked ham until crisp.

2 Remove from the pan with a slotted spoon and set aside to cool.

3 Add the chicory to the pan, cook gently until softened, then tip into a food processor or blender.

4 Pour in the milk, add the gingerbread and crème fraîche and whiz until smooth.

5 Pour into a saucepan, bring to a boil and simmer for 10 minutes.

6 Cool, then chill in the fridge.

7 Serve scattered with the smoked ham.

You'll get a day's dose of **vitamin C** from one kiwi fruit, plus unique **phytochemicals** to protect DNA and enormous antioxidant properties from **betacarotene** and other nutrients. Kiwi fruit are essential for recovery from respiratory problems, particularly for children.

cold and fizzy kiwi

Here's a restorative soup that's ready in minutes. It may sound like a smoothie, but I was served this as a cold soup before a meal of what my wife described as the best mussels she'd ever eaten. We were on the edge of Coramandel Bay in New Zealand, where the best kiwi fruit and green-lipped mussels come from. Our hostess used local red apples, but the tang of a crisp Cox or Granny Smith gives a much better flavour.

kiwi fruit 6, peeled and roughly chopped
apples 2, peeled, cored and roughly chopped
crème fraîche 300ml or 10fl oz
caster sugar 100g or 3½oz
lemonade 150ml or 5fl oz good-quality fizzy, preferably home-made

1 Put the fruit, crème fraîche and sugar into a food processor or blender and whiz until smooth.

2 Leave in the fridge to chill.

3 Add the lemonade just before serving and mix well.

good-mood soups

It's a sad fact of modern life that few people realize how their eating habits affect their moods. In 2000, I wrote a whole book about good-mood foods and although the public loved it and it was hugely successful (translated into several languages), the medical world was generally more cynical. Some people happily accept that too much alcohol makes you depressed, that too much coffee makes you agitated, that eating magic mushrooms makes you happy. Yet they find it so hard to believe that the essential oils in basil are calming and that lime-blossom tea makes you sleepy.

The proof of the pudding, as they say, is in the eating, so try it yourself. Every one of these soups tastes great, which means you won't need teaspoons of sugar to help these medicines go down. Apart from the possibility of some flatulence from the Jerusalem artichokes in Pasta, Pear and Blue Cheese (*see* page 76), feeling a bit sleepy after Spiced Lettuce with Goat's Cheese (opposite) and slightly garlicky breath after Alli-Um-Yum (*see* page 73), there are no side effects.

In fact, Alli-Um-Yum combines four of the most powerful members of the allium family. In terms of overall health promotion, this blockbuster will help fight raised cholesterol, increased blood pressure and the risk of blood clots that can lead to strokes. In winter, some of the most common causes of misery and depression are a chronic cough, repeated colds and endless bouts of flu. This recipe will help you feel good by fighting against these seasonal infections.

Nothing puts you in a bad mood as easily as chronic pain, perhaps caused by arthritis and other joint problems. Anyone suffering from arthritis, rheumatism, gout or muscle pain will benefit from Coriander and Sweet Cherry Soup (*see* page 77). Similarly, a lack of iron is a frequent cause of anaemia, which results in exhaustion, irritability and depression. And a lack of vitamin B_6 is a common factor in the emotional peaks and troughs and heightened agitation that occur in women with severe PMS. You can give these missing nutrients an instant boost with a bowl of my Cornmeal with Scallops soup (*see* page 75).

Whatever your mood, whatever your situation, whatever your preferences, you'll find more than one recipe in this chapter to suit you. All the soups are good sources of health-giving nutrients and are low or very low in saturated fat, salt and other unhealthy ingredients. They can't do you or your family anything but good.

All lettuces provide small amounts of morphine-like chemicals that help you relax, as well as a little **vitamin C** and **betacarotene**. Goat's cheese is rich in **calcium**, **protein** and **vitamin B$_2$** and a good source of **tryptophan**, a key good-mood nutrient.

spiced lettuce soup with goat's cheese

If insomnia is your problem, this soup is a better remedy than all but the most powerful of pills. What's more, it makes you feel good, it's highly protective and helps keep bones strong and healthy. Although any lettuce will do, the darker the leaves, the higher the content of valuable nutrients – especially betacarotene – you'll get.

butter 25g or 1oz, unsalted

onion 1, finely chopped

garlic 1 clove, smashed and finely chopped

cumin 1 teaspoon, ground

pepper 1 small green, deseeded and very finely chopped

lettuce 1 large (any type), roughly shredded

vegetable stock 1.5 litres or 51fl oz – *see* page 104 or use a good stock cube or bouillon powder

goat's cheese 150g or 5½oz, soft, finely diced

1 Melt the butter in a large saucepan and gently sauté the onions and garlic for 5 minutes.

2 Sprinkle in the cumin, stir thoroughly and cook for 2 more minutes.

3 Add the pepper, lettuce and stock and simmer for 5 minutes.

4 Whiz in a food processor or blender – or use a hand blender – until smooth, then return to the saucepan to heat through.

5 Serve hot with the diced cheese on top.

vital statistics

This soup provides a little **iron** and **vitamin C** and very few calories. **Lentinan**, which fights cancer cells and **eritadenine** to help lower cholesterol are both present in mushrooms. **Calcium** is provided by the cheese and crème fraîche.

very different mushroom soup

An old Spanish proverb says: 'Between soup and love, the first is better.' That's certainly true of this mood-enhancing mushroom mixture. All mushrooms are healthy, as they're fat-free, low in calories and a good source of nutrients. In Chinese and Japanese medicine, mushrooms are revered as medicinal treatments: shiitake for immunity, reishi for the liver and asthma, maitake for blood pressure and liver disease. The combination of mushrooms with cheese is a certain mood-booster.

butter 25g or 1oz, unsalted

onion 1, finely chopped

shiitake mushrooms 600g or 1lb 5oz, finely chopped

flour 1 heaped tablespoon

vegetable stock 1 litre or 34fl oz – *see* page 104 or use a good stock cube or bouillon powder

manchega cheese about 150g or 5oz

crème fraîche 200ml or 7fl oz, half-fat

1 Heat the butter in a large saucepan.

2 Add the onions and mushrooms and sauté gently, stirring continuously, until the onions are soft and golden.

3 Sprinkle on the flour, mix well and continue cooking, stirring continuously, for 2 minutes.

4 Pour in the stock, stir and simmer for 20 minutes.

5 Add the cheese and the crème fraîche. Stir well and continue cooking for 2 more minutes, until the cheese has softened.

6 Whiz in a food processor or blender – or use a hand blender – until smooth. Serve garnished with extra fried mushrooms if you wish.

Chestnuts aren't rich in **protein**, but they do provide **vitamins B$_1$, B$_2$** and the PMS-relieving B$_6$. They're also a good source of **potassium**. The pancetta provides some protein and salt, so don't add extra salt.

chestnut soup

Apart from stuffing the Christmas turkey and burning your fingers when you roast a few, chestnuts are underused and seriously underrated. Unlike most other nuts, they're virtually fat-free and have only 170 calories per 100g or 3^1/$_2$oz. They make great gluten-free flour and also purée – as used in this recipe. Their delicious taste disguises their nerve-nourishing vitamin B content. With a little butter, a dollop of crème fraîche and a splash of cognac, of course this soup will make you feel good.

butter 10g or ^{1}/$_4$oz, unsalted

onion 1 medium, very finely chopped

garlic 1 clove, smashed and very finely chopped

chestnut purée 500g or 1lb 2oz

beef stock 1.5 litres or 54fl oz – *see* page 105 or use a good stock cube or bouillon powder

crème fraîche 100ml or 3^1/$_2$fl oz

cognac 3 tablespoons

pancetta 200g or 7oz, grilled until crisp

1 Melt the butter in a large saucepan and gently sauté the onion and garlic until softened.

2 Tip in the chestnut purée and stock and stir well.

3 Add the cream and cognac and bring to a simmer.

4 Crumble the pancetta on top to serve.

alli-um-yum

vital statistics

All the alliums provide **phytochemicals** that help reduce cholesterol, lower blood pressure, lessen the risk of blood clots and boost natural resistance to bacterial and fungal infections. Lemon balm (*Melissa*), a member of the mint family, contains mood-enhancing **essential oils**.

Thirty years ago, garlic was thought of as something only 'foreigners' ate – so much so that, because I recommended it so often, I was nicknamed 'Dr Garlic' by a leading UK political broadcaster at the station where I began my radio career. Today, I'm sure that most of my readers know about the heart-protective and cholesterol- and infection-fighting properties of this amazing bulb. What may be a surprise is the idea that garlic and its relatives from the allium family, combined with lemon balm, make this a great mood-enhancing recipe.

onions 2 medium, finely chopped

leeks 2, finely sliced

spring onions 3 large, finely sliced

garlic 2 cloves, smashed and finely chopped

ginger root 2.5cm or 1in fresh, grated

vegetable stock 1.2 litres or 40fl oz – *see* page 104 or use a good stock cube or bouillon powder

soy sauce 5 tablespoons

lemon balm 1 tablespoon, fresh, finely chopped

1 Put the onions, leeks, spring onions, garlic and ginger in a large saucepan.

2 Just cover with water and simmer for 5 minutes.

3 Add the stock and soy sauce and simmer for 45 minutes, adding extra water if necessary.

4 Whiz in a food processor or blender until smooth.

5 Sprinkle with the lemon balm to serve.

michael's tip

It's unlikely that you'll find lemon balm in your supermarket, but there will be lots in your local garden centre. Buy a pot and either transfer it to a larger pot or plant it inside an old bucket in the ground to prevent it taking over your garden. Lemon balm makes great tea and is also a powerful remedy for the relief and prevention of cold sores: make tea and dab it on, or crush the leaves and put them on your lips.

vital statistics

Just 100g or 3^1/$_2$oz of cornmeal provides 30 per cent of a day's supply of B$_6$, 38 per cent of fibre, 20 per cent of protein, 20 per cent of thiamine and around 25 per cent of iron, magnesium, zinc and manganese. Scallops boost the protein, zinc and iron content and add omega-3 fatty acids.

cornmeal with scallops

Cornmeal is a traditional food of Native Americans, both north and south. Not widely used in the UK and the rest of northern Europe, it's popularly known as polenta in Italy. It makes an excellent base for this good-mood soup, thanks to its B vitamins and tryptophan. Like all shellfish, scallops provide minerals and essential fatty acids: both important brain foods.

milk 1 litre or 34fl oz, full-fat

yellow cornmeal 450g or 1lb

potato 1 medium, peeled and finely diced

garlic 2 cloves, smashed and finely chopped

sage 1 large sprig, fresh

potato flour 1 tablespoon

butter 25g or 1oz, unsalted

scallops 4

1 Put the milk into a large saucepan and add the cornmeal, potatoes, garlic and sage.

2 Simmer for 20 minutes, stirring occasionally, until the potatoes are soft.

3 Remove the sage.

4 Purée using a hand blender, then sieve into a clean saucepan.

5 Sprinkle on the potato flour and reheat, stirring.

6 Melt the butter in a large saucepan.

7 Cut the scallops into quarters (or 6 or 8 pieces if large) and cook in the butter until firm – about 45 seconds.

8 Put the soup into individual serving bowls and place the scallop pieces on top.

pasta, pear and blue cheese

At times of stress, carbohydrates can help stimulate the release of relaxing, feel-good brain chemicals. But they do need to be complex carbs: those with the lowest glycaemic index. This recipe has low-GI carbs in abundance from the pasta, artichokes and parsnips. Also featuring the mood-boosting effects of ginger, this is a stress-busting, feel-good soup.

olive oil 2 tablespoons

shallots 2, finely chopped

ginger root 2.5cm or 1in fresh, grated

parsnip 1 medium, finely cubed

carrot 1, trimmed and peeled if not organic (organics just need to be scrubbed), diced

jerusalem artichokes 5, finely cubed

pears 2 large, sliced

chicken or vegetable stock 1 litre or 34fl oz – *see* pages 106 and 104 or use a good stock cube or bouillon powder

crème fraîche 200ml or 7fl oz, low-fat

blue cheese 150g or 5½oz, crumbled

tiny pasta such as farfalle, 150g or 5½oz

1 Put the oil into a large saucepan. Add the shallots and ginger and sauté gently until the shallots are soft and golden.

2 Add the vegetables, pears and stock, bring to a boil then reduce the heat and simmer for 30 minutes.

3 Add the crème fraîche and cheese and whiz in a food processor or blender – or use a hand blender – until smooth.

4 Pour back into the pan, add the pasta and leave off the heat until the pasta is cooked – about 10 minutes, depending on the type of pasta.

vital statistics

Cherries are a rich source of **potassium**, with almost no sodium, making them a perfect fruit for anyone with high blood pressure or heart disease. They have significant amounts of protective **bioflavonoids** and **ellagic acid**, which adds to their anti-cancer properties.

coriander and sweet cherry soup

When it comes to feeling good, a drop of cherry brandy can't hurt, but the cherries themselves in this unusual Middle Eastern soup have extraordinary healing powers and are pretty near the top of the list of protective foods. They probably started life in Mesopotamia and were used medicinally by Ancient Greek physicians. Anyone suffering from arthritis, rheumatism, gout or muscle pain will benefit from this soup.

ground coriander 1 heaped teaspoon

runny honey 2 tablespoons

cherries 400g or 14oz, sweet, stones removed

crème fraîche 100ml or 3½fl oz

milk 600ml or 20fl oz, organic

cherry brandy 2 tablespoons (optional)

coriander leaves about 10 fresh, finely chopped

1 Mix together the ground coriander and honey.

2 Put into a food processor or blender, add the cherries, crème fraîche, milk and cherry brandy (if using) and whiz until smooth.

3 Leave to chill thoroughly in the fridge.

4 Serve with the coriander leaves on top.

slimming soups

Obesity is a growing problem in the UK, America and Europe. Even where the traditional Mediterranean diet has helped maintain a high level of public health, the relentless march of burgers, fried chicken and other fast food, combined with the worldwide spread of canned drinks and convenience foods high in fat, salt, sugar and refined carbohydrates, is adding to the weight of nations.

I've never been a fan of extreme slimming diets, much preferring the old-fashioned approach of healthy food, less of it and more exercise as the most accessible form of weight loss. Yet, when obesity is costing the NHS hundreds of millions of pounds a year for the treatment of all of the joint, heart, breathing and circulatory problems it causes, it's time to take notice. When children of seven, eight and nine develop type-2 diabetes, a disease historically seen in the overweight and middle-aged, we must take action.

There are no shortcuts, no magic pills and no diet gurus who will make it easy for you to lose weight. Most slimming pills and potions, diet foods, magic wraps, hot-stone massages and 'world-famous' diet clinics will, in the long term, remove more pounds from your pocket than from your body. Even liposuction and plastic surgery reverse themselves in time; I've had many people phone one of my radio programmes desperate for help after gastric by-pass operations. They often seem unaware of the real consequences and side-effects caused by the non-absorption of nutrients – or of how little they'll be able to eat and the huge price of lost pleasure this surgery entails.

None of these soups consumed in isolation will help you lose a single ounce, but if you use them as a substitute for one meal a day for anything from one to eight weeks, you will lose weight if the rest of your diet is sensible.

The combination of instant and slow-release energy in Perfect Potage (*see* page 85), makes it an ideal lunch for a busy day. Veggie Soup with Tofu (opposite) is not only a nutritious low-calorie super soup, but ideal to help you cope with PMS, irregular periods, or menopausal symptoms. The barley in Herb Broth (*see* page 82), combined with the meatballs, is a source of muscle-building protein and restorative energy – the perfect evening meal after a strenuous workout in the gym. Finally, take a tip from the Nobel Prize-winning scientist Ilya Mechnikov and make sure you get the calcium and immunity-boosting bacteria from Bulgarian Chicken Soup with Yogurt (*see* page 88).

Protein and very important plant hormones are provided by tofu. Aubergines are a member of the nightshade family (like potatoes and tomatoes) and contain lots of **vitamins** and **minerals**, but it's the special protective plant chemicals in the skin that are very special. Most important is **nasunin**, which specifically protects the fats on the surface of brain cells.

veggie soup with tofu

Miso is a fermented soya-bean paste from Japan. It's now so popular that you'll find it in most supermarkets. It's basically a seasoning, but with a difference: it's extremely rich in some nutrients. Usually made from soya beans, some varieties are based on wheat, rice or barley. There's no doubt, however, that soya has immense health benefits: just 35g or a generous ounce is a very good source of the feel-good chemicals tryptophan and manganese and an even better source of copper, zinc, protein and vitamin K (essential for blood clotting). But read the labels – some cheap varieties contain the dreaded MSG (monosodiumglutamate). Tofu is often promoted as a good source of vitamin B_{12} for vegetarians and vegans, but researchers and UK Government tables disagree about the amount it contains.

miso 5 tablespoons

carrots 2, trimmed and peeled if not organic (organics just need to be scrubbed), diced

aubergine 1 large, unpeeled and diced

tofu 175g or 6oz, cubed

1 Bring 1.2 litres or 40fl oz of water to a boil.

2 Add the miso and mix well to dissolve.

3 Add the carrots, aubergines and tofu and simmer until the vegetables are tender.

vital statistics

You'll get valuable **selenium**, **fibre**, **copper** and **manganese** from the barley, antibacterial phytochemicals in the onion and leek, and diuretic effects from the parsley. The meatballs provide extra **protein**, **iron** and **B vitamins**.

herb broth

The great chef Auguste Escoffier says: 'Soup puts the heart at ease, calms the violence of hunger, eliminates the tension of the day and awakens and refines the appetite.' That's just what you need if you're trying to follow a weight-loss regime. If this soup is a starter, have it on its own if you're serious about weight loss. Adding the meatballs makes it a substantial and satisfying meal with a low total calorie count and plenty of slow-release energy, thanks to the barley and the protein in the meatballs. Barley is now sadly neglected, but the Ancient Romans knew it to be a real body-building food. The oldest of cultivated cereals, it's high in fibre and low in calories.

onion 1 small, finely chopped
leek 1, finely chopped
pearl barley 4 tablespoons
lettuce half a small head, chopped
watercress 1 large handful, chopped
sorrel 1 large handful, chopped
flat-leaf parsley 1 large handful, chopped

1 Put all the ingredients into a large saucepan.

2 Cover with 1.5 litres or 51fl oz water.

3 Simmer for 50 minutes.

michael's tip

To make this soup more substantial, try it with the meatball recipe on page 107.

vital statistics

Spinach is a rich source of eye-protective carotenoids as well as betacarotene. Although it contains lots of iron, very little of it is absorbed during digestion. Like all root vegetables, celeriac is an excellent source of minerals, especially potassium (for blood-pressure reduction). It also provides folic acid, fibre and vitamins B_1, B_6, C and K.

low-fat summer's dream

This soup is really low-fat! In fact, apart from the very small amount of healthy natural oils in the pine nuts, it's no-fat. I think that many soups are delicious when left with some crunch in them, but this is one that really needs to be the smoothest purée. I top it with the toasted pine nuts because I love the taste and they're good for you.

leek 1 large, sliced
celeriac 1 large, peeled and diced
spinach 500g or 1lb 2oz fresh, young
white wine 250g or 9fl oz, dry
nutmeg freshly grated
pine nuts 2 tablespoons

1 Put the leek, celeriac and spinach in a large saucepan.

2 Pour in the wine and 250ml or 9fl oz water and bring to a boil.

3 Simmer for 15 to 20 minutes, or until the celeriac is soft.

4 Whiz in a food processor or blender – or use a hand blender – until smooth.

5 Taste, season and stir in the nutmeg. Keep warm.

6 Dry-fry the pine nuts until golden.

7 Serve the soup with the pine nuts scattered on top.

michael's tip

Great, big, knobbly celeriac can be hell to peel. Save a lot of time and bad language by using a large, very sharp knife and cutting it into a skinless cube.

vital statistics

Celery and parsley both help eliminate excess fluid. Carrots provide masses of immunity-boosting and skin-friendly **betacarotene**. As well as being a slimming aid, this recipe has diuretic properties thatcan help ease the discomfort of premenstrual fluid retention.

perfect potage

If you're going to use soup to help you with your slimming programme, this is a pretty good place to start. Although it is a filling and substantial soup, it's low in calories and virtually fat-free. Thanks to the natural sugar content of the carrots, you'll get instant energy, plus the benefits of slow-release energy from the vegetable fibre and the rice.

carrots 3 large, trimmed and peeled if not organic (organics just need to be scrubbed), sliced

celery 2 stalks, sliced

onion 1 medium, finely sliced

long-grain rice 50g or 2oz

vegetable stock 1.2 litres or 40fl oz – *see* page 104 or use a good stock cube or bouillon powder

bouquet garni 1

parsley 4 tablespoons, finely chopped

1 Put the carrots, celery, onion and rice into a large saucepan.

2 Add about half the stock and the bouquet garni, bring to a boil and simmer until the vegetables are tender – about 20 minutes. Remove the bouquet garni.

3 Whiz in a food processor or blender – or use a hand blender – until smooth.

4 Pour back into the saucepan and add the rest of the stock.

5 Sprinkle on the parsley to serve.

vital statistics

Iodine in the fish stimulates the thyroid. Traditional curry spices help boost circulation and metabolism. You get extra calcium and B vitamins from the yogurt.

curried fish and herb

Here's a very low-fat, spicy soup that makes a great one-pot meal for slimmers. Low in calories, rich in nutrients, substantial and filling, this would make a perfect evening meal followed by a salad, some fresh fruit and 50g or about 2oz of low-fat cheese. Dieting can be stressful, and this combination of nutrients helps fight the stress as well as the flab.

butter 10g or ¼oz, unsalted

onion 1, very finely chopped

curry powder 1 tablespoon

white fish 350g or 12oz firm, cut into small chunks

thyme 1 sprig

parsley 1 sprig

bay leaf 1

saffron 1 pinch

fish stock 1.2 litres or 40fl oz – *see* page 104 or use a good stock cube or bouillon powder

low-fat yogurt about 250ml or 9fl oz

1 Melt the butter in a large saucepan. Add the onions and sauté gently until soft and golden.

2 Sprinkle on the curry powder and continue cooking for 2 minutes, stirring thoroughly so that the curry powder is well combined.

3 Add the fish, the herbs and spices and the fish stock.

4 Bring to a boil and simmer for 10 minutes, or until the fish is cooked.

5 Fish out the bay leaf and the woody herbs.

6 Add the yogurt and stir carefully, without breaking up the fish.

vital statistics

A nutrient-dense recipe containing plenty of basic **vitamins** and **minerals** from the vegetables, protective **antioxidants** from the onion and leek, immunity-boosting friendly bacteria from the yogurt, and the magical chicken ingredient that kills germs.

bulgarian chicken soup with yogurt

The Russian scientist Ilya Mechnikov, who won the 1908 Nobel Prize for physiology and medicine, concluded that the remarkably long life span of Bulgarian peasants was due to the traditional inclusion of live yogurt in their daily food. I'm sure he'd have loved this soup, not only for its distinctly European flavour, but also for the inclusion of yogurt, which so fascinated him during his research career.

butter 50g or 2oz, unsalted

onion 1, finely chopped

leek 1, finely chopped

new potatoes 3, finely cubed

celery 2 sticks, finely diced

carrot 1, trimmed and peeled if not organic (organics just need to be scrubbed), finely cubed

chicken 2 skinless breasts, cut finely into strips

chicken stock 1.5 litres or 51fl oz – *see* page 106 or use a good stock cube or bouillon powder

flat-leaf parsley 1 handful, chopped, stalks removed

greek yogurt 4 large spoonfuls, 0 per cent fat

1 Put the butter in a large saucepan and gently sauté the onions and leeks until soft.

2 Add the rest of the vegetables and the chicken and continue cooking, stirring constantly, until the chicken is golden – about 5 minutes.

3 Add the stock and parsley and simmer for about 20 minutes or until the vegetables and chicken are cooked through and tender.

4 Serve with a spoonful of yogurt in each bowl.

vital statistics

This light, clear soup benefits from the **minerals** and **vitamins** leached out of the vegetables during cooking. It's a low-calorie soup that you can make even lower by refrigerating overnight and removing any fat from the surface before reheating the next day.

quick consommé

I always think it's such a shame that people don't bother to make consommés at home, especially when they're so popular on restaurant menus, so simple and so nutritious. Any decent cookbook written before the 1960s would have had them in the 'sickroom cooking' section. As part of your weight-loss regime, there would be very little fat from the lean beef and giblets – even less if they're organic.

beef about 450g or 1lb, lean

chicken giblets a few (optional)

leek 1, finely chopped

carrot 1, trimmed and peeled if not organic (organics just need to be scrubbed), roughly diced

celery 1 stick, finely sliced

lettuce 1, roughly chopped

onion 1, left whole

cloves 2

chervil a handful, fresh

peppercorns 1 level teaspoon

1 Put the beef and chicken giblets (if using) into a large saucepan with the vegetables, cloves, chervil and peppercorns.

2 Pour on 2 litres or 68fl oz of water and stir until boiling.

3 Simmer gently for about 50 minutes.

4 Leave to cool slightly, skim and strain – preferably through muslin.

michael's tip

This simple soup is so versatile. To make it more substantial, try it with any of the garnishes on pages 107–109, add 2 tablespoons of tomato purée, or just bring it to a simmer and use to poach eggs.

sexy soups

Today, as sperm counts plummet, women's fertility declines and the number of couples unable to conceive rockets, it seems beyond belief to me that so few couples are ever asked about their diets or given advice on the simple changes that could resolve their problems before resorting to high-tech methods. The same is true for loss of libido and erectile dysfunction: the 'easy answer' is drugs with side effects, but the real long-term solution starts with better nutrition.

Women who diet to lose weight are likely to have a poor nutrition intake, whether it's a 'thousand-calorie' diet, the cabbage-soup diet, the Atkins diet, or any other extreme weight-loss regime. Lack of essential nutrients can have catastrophic effects on the body's ability to reproduce – and, whether it's men or women, it can be equally disastrous when it comes to enjoying a regular, active sex life.

It often seems to be the women who bear the brunt of tests, investigations and treatments when conception becomes a problem, but it's just as often the men who are having difficulties. For the male half of the equation, the solutions are usually much cheaper and much simpler and they can be dramatically effective. Miracles don't happen overnight, however, and whether your problems are failing to conceive, erectile disfunction or simply the absence of the spark that ignites your passions, be patient and add these soups to your regular diet.

For something really different, just think of those beautiful tennis players when you enjoy Love All (*see* page 97), but if your tastes run to the more traditional, then the simple version of the classic Bouillabaisse (*see* page 96) just oozes sensuality – and much more besides.

'Bouillabaisse ... this incomparable golden soup, which embodies and concentrates all the aromas of our shores and which permeates like an ecstasy the stomachs of astonished gastronomes. Bouillabaisse is one of those classic dishes whose glory has encircled the world and the miracle consists of this: there are as many bouillabaisses as there are good chefs. Each brings to his own version his special touch.'

So said the great French 'Prince of Gastronomes', Curnonsky (Maurice Edmond Sailland), a passionate supporter of traditional French provincial cooking. No doubt you will bring your own special – and romantic – touch to this soup, too.

vital statistics

Fish stock offers plenty of **minerals** and **B vitamins**, while prawns provide **protein**, **zinc** and **selenium**. The spices in curry powder stimulate circulation. Coconut milk adds the sensuous perfume of the tropics.

curried coconut

There's nothing quite so romantic or sexy as images of tropical islands, coconut palms and blue seas. It only takes a hint of coconut aroma to transport us to sun-drenched tropical shores. For years, coconut and coconut oil have been thought of as unhealthy, whereas the opposite is the truth. There is saturated fat in coconut, but 60 per cent is the healthiest type, easily digested and quickly converted into energy. These fats protect the circulation because they don't end up as fatty deposits in the arteries. Add the natural aphrodisiacs in the prawns, with the exotic hint of curry – what more could you desire?

olive oil 2 tablespoons

shallots 2 large (or 3 small)

garlic 2 cloves, smashed and finely chopped

curry powder 1 tablespoon

coconut milk 300ml or 10fl oz

fish stock 700ml or 24fl oz – *see* page 104 or use a good stock cube or bouillon powder

crème fraîche 100ml or 3½fl oz

lemon liqueur 4 tablespoons (optional)

prawns 12, cooked and peeled

1 Heat the oil in a large saucepan. Add the shallots and garlic, sprinkle on the curry powder, mix well and sauté gently until the shallots are soft.

2 Add the coconut milk and stock, bring to a boil and simmer for 5 minutes.

3 Add the crème fraîche.

4 Blend until smooth, either in a food processor or blender or with a hand blender.

5 Cool, then chill well in the fridge.

6 Before serving, stir in the lemon liqueur, if using.

7 Serve with the prawns scattered on top.

turmeric, ginger and acorn squash

The great 18th century British wit (and clergyman) Dr Sydney Smith wrote a great deal about food. One of my favourite quotes is: 'Soup and fish explain half the emotions of human life.' When it comes to the emotions of sex, this soup is a winner. The stimulus of ginger, the spice of turmeric and the heat of curry, all combined with the exotic and romantic flavours of coconut, are almost guaranteed to make this dish an enjoyable aphrodisiac.

vegetable stock 1 litre or 34fl oz – *see* page 104 or use a good stock cube or bouillon powder

onion 1 medium, finely sliced

garlic 2 large cloves, smashed and finely chopped

ginger root 2.5cm or 1in fresh, grated

turmeric 1 teaspoon

curry powder 1 teaspoon

squash or pumpkin flesh, about 700g or 1lb 9oz, cubed

coconut milk about 250ml or 9fl oz

1 Put 1 tablespoon of the stock in a large saucepan.

2 Add the onion, bring to a simmer and cook for 5 minutes, stirring occasionally.

3 Add the garlic and ginger and cook for 2 more minutes.

4 Add the turmeric and curry powder and mix well.

5 Pour in the rest of the stock and add the squash or pumpkin flesh.

6 Bring to a simmer and cook until the vegetables are tender – about 10 minutes.

7 Stir in the coconut milk.

8 Whiz in a food processor or blender until smooth.

vital statistics

Prawns are an excellent source of protein, vitamins and minerals: vitamin B_{12} for healthy blood, iodine for your thyroid, zinc and selenium for fertility and a healthy prostate.

simple bouillabaisse

Bouillabaisse is a miracle, and one that you can produce easily in your own kitchen. Fish is always a good choice as a prelude to romance: it's light and easily digested. Fish, and especially shellfish, contain nutrients essential for sexual performance. There is energy for physical activity, protection for the circulation and nutrients to enhance sensuality.

good olive oil 3 tablespoons

onion 1 medium, finely chopped

fennel bulb 1 medium, very finely chopped

garlic 2 cloves, smashed and finely chopped

new potatoes 3 medium, cubed

fish stock 1.5 litres or 51fl oz – *see* page 104 or use a good stock cube or bouillon powder

lemon zest from 1 lemon

tomato purée 2 tablespoons

bouquet garni 1

white fish 450g or 1lb, mixed (halibut, turbot, etc), cut into 2.5cm or 1in cubes

prawns 12, peeled

1 Heat the oil in a large, wide saucepan.

2 Soften the onion, fennel and garlic in the pan.

3 Add the potatoes and stir until they're covered with the oil.

4 Pour in the stock, add the lemon zest, tomato purée and bouquet garni and simmer for 20 minutes.

5 Add the fish and prawns and continue cooking for another 10 minutes.

vital statistics

Exhaustion and sex aren't good bedfellows, but strawberries contain a little iron and masses of vitamin C to help anaemia. They also reduce joint pain, protect against viruses and ward off heart and circulatory disease. A little alcohol from the champagne is an instant mood-enhancer.

love all

Chilled soups, like vichyssoise and borscht, aren't unusual, but they're cooked, then chilled – unlike traditional Turkish or Middle Eastern yogurt-based soups, which are uncooked. Strangely, the traditional fruit soups so popular in parts of Eastern Europe have not been popular on restaurant menus until very recently. Here, we have the unrivalled aphrodisiac combination of strawberries and cream with champagne – already an established favourite at Wimbledon, where 'love' is in the air...

strawberries 450g or 1lb, hulled
icing sugar 50g or 2oz
single cream 150ml or 5fl oz
lemon zest from 1 lemon
champagne or sparkling wine, 200ml or 7fl oz

1 Put the strawberries, sugar and cream into a food processor or blender and whiz until smooth.

2 Add the lemon zest, mix well and leave in the fridge until well chilled.

3 Just before serving, pour in the champagne or sparkling wine and mix well.

tango with mango

Here's another exotic soup to conjure up the romance of the tropics. With the traditional aphrodisiac properties of mango, the passion of passion fruit and chocolate, the original food of love, how could this one fail? It was originally reserved for the Aztec royal family and it's no accident that the botanical genus name for the cocoa tree is *Theobroma*, meaning 'food of the Gods'.

cane sugar about 150g or 5½oz
mango 3 large, ripe, peeled, stones removed and cut into very small dice. (Keep any juices that try to escape.)
white rum 4 tablespoons
passion fruit 2
good dark chocolate 8 squares – minimum 70% cocoa solids, grated

1 Put 850ml or 29fl oz of water into a large saucepan. Add the sugar, stir well and heat very gently for 10 minutes, until dissolved.

2 Tip in the mango and any reserved juices and continue cooking for 5 more minutes. Leave to cool.

3 Pour in the rum, mix well and leave in the fridge for at least 8 hours.

4 Take the flesh out of the passion fruit, mix with the mango and put into serving bowls.

5 Serve with the grated chocolate scattered on top.

basics and garnishes

Years ago, my great friend the chef Raymond Blanc told me that with two carrots, an onion and a handful of fresh herbs, he could make a soup fit for the Queen. How right he was! The wonderful thing about making soup is that you can use almost anything left in the fridge, the pantry, the vegetable patch or the freezer. The traditional Brussels sprouts and Stilton from the Christmas leftovers, chicken soup from the remains of Sunday lunch with a few leaves of kale, a couple of turnips you didn't cook, the half red pepper that didn't get used in the salad and maybe the handful of frozen soya beans at the bottom of the bag ... use them all to make up your own combinations.

The only things you must have are a chopping board, a good sharp knife and a large, thick-bottomed saucepan. A large strainer is useful, and a proper stockpot with a strainer basket makes life much easier. Although you don't *need* anything sophisticated, it's worth investing some money if you plan to be a regular soup-maker. Modern technology really helps.

knives

Good kitchen shops and even supermarkets these days have quite impressive ranges of quality kitchen knives. There are also speciality mail-order companies that deal in kitchen equipment. The great revolution since the original *Super Soups* book has been the Internet, where you can find the best products at the best prices and purchase online. Of all the knives I've tried, there's no doubt that by far the best are made in Japan of multilayered hardened steel; they're razor-sharp and keep their edge for ages. They are the most expensive, but if you look after them, they're a really worthwhile investment. And as any chef will tell you, it's *blunt* knives that cause accidents. Try www.lakeland.co.uk.

food processors and blenders

The cheap, old-fashioned, hand-turned Mouli-légumes, a French kitchen gadget from the 1940s, is a quick and easy way to make soups, sauces, purées and baby food. It costs around £12–£25, depending on size. Again, try Lakeland. On the next step up are the brilliant hand-held miniature processors. Hand blenders can cost as little as £10, but by far the best is the Swiss-made Bamix, which liquidizes, blends, chops, whisks and grinds. It's not cheap at around £90, but it lasts forever and is incredibly quick and versatile – and easy to clean.

If you want the Rolls-Royce of blenders, the American retro Kitchen-Aid is the best, but also the most expensive at around £120 – www.decuisine.co.uk.

The one machine that does everything is the MagiMix Food Processor. The latest models are better than ever. Because they're multipurpose, however, they can be a bit more fiddly and take a bit more cleaning. These are priced from £150, depending on size; again, I recommend Lakeland.

taking stock

There's no doubt that home-made stock is the be-all and end-all of a good soup. Yes, it seems time-consuming to make, but it really is worth the effort. I normally set aside a couple of hours on a Sunday morning or evening when I can watch something silly on telly or listen to my favourite music while the stock simmers away.

If you haven't got time, there are now – happily – bouillon powders and cubes that are okay, and 'fresh' stock in the supermarket chiller cabinets. I haven't found one that isn't salty, however, and I still believe that making your own is the best. And it's easy.

Make friends with your butcher (supermarkets these days have very experienced professionals) and give him or her a few days' notice when you want, say, some beef, lamb, pork or ham bones. You can now also get veal bones, thanks to the more humane farming methods of breeding and raising young cattle. The same goes for your fishmonger; when they fillet fish for other people, ask them to save the bones for you – they'll only go in the bin, after all. But if you use them to make stock for the fish recipes in this book, you'll get some wonderful flavours that are a million times more satisfying than using stock cubes.

Another good thing about making your own stock is that it's so easy to freeze. Just use the quantities listed here, then boil until reduced by half, cool and pour into ice-cube trays. When you need perhaps just 10ml or $^1/_3$oz of stock to add to a fish dish, 100ml or $3^1/_2$oz for a risotto or a bit more for a stew, you can simply tip them out into a bowl and add boiling water to dissolve them and take them back to your desired strength.

fish stock

fish trimmings and bones

about 100g or 3½oz. Most supermarkets that offer a filleting service will keep bones, heads and trimmings if given a day's notice. Better still, find an independent fishmonger who will almost certainly do it for you.

carrots 3, trimmed, peeled if not organic (organics just need to be scrubbed), and cubed

onions 2 sweet white Spanish, chopped

leek 1 large, washed and chopped

rosemary 1 large sprig

parsley 1 medium bunch

mint 1 medium bunch

tarragon 3 large sprigs

water and/or dry white wine or a mixture of both 1 litre or 34fl oz

white peppercorns 8

salt about ½ teaspoon

1 Put the washed and dried fish trimmings in a large saucepan.

2 Add the rest of the ingredients and bring to the boil slowly.

3 Simmer for about 60 to 75 minutes, skimming the surface regularly.

4 Strain through a kitchen muslin or fine sieve.

vegetable stock

onions 2, 1 peeled and quartered, 1 left whole with the skin on (for colour)

celery 3 large stalks

leek 1 large stalk, cleaned and sliced

parsnip 1 large bulb, trimmed, peeled if not organic (organics just need to be scrubbed)

mushrooms 3 large, chopped roughly

sage 1 large sprig

thyme 2 sprigs

bay leaves 6

parsley 1 small bunch

water about 1 litre or 34fl oz

peppercorns 8

salt about ½ teaspoon

1 Put all the ingredients into a large saucepan – or, ideally, a pasta pan with a fitted sieve.

2 Bring to the boil slowly.

3 Simmer for about 60 to 75 minutes.

4 Remove the pasta sieve or strain through a kitchen muslin or sieve.

beef, lamb or pork stock

meat bones about 900g or 2lb, chopped into 4cm or 1½in pieces by your butcher

onions 2 large, red, peeled and coarsely chopped

carrots 2 large, trimmed, peeled if not organic (organics just need to be scrubbed)

leek 1 large, chopped coarsely

celery 2 large sticks, chopped

sage 1 large bunch

rosemary 1 sprig

bay leaves 5

peppercorns 10

water 2 litres or 68fl oz

salt about ½ teaspoon

1 Roast the meat bones for about 30 minutes at 220°C or 425°F or gas mark 7.

2 Put them and any scrapings into a large saucepan.

3 Add the rest of the ingredients.

4 Bring to the boil and simmer slowly for about 4 hours, skimming regularly with a slotted spoon to remove the fat.

5 Strain through a kitchen muslin or sieve.

6 Leave, covered, until completely cold.

7 Skim off any solidified fat.

ham stock

ham bones about 900g or 2lb

onions 2 large, red, peeled and coarsely chopped

carrots 2 large, trimmed, peeled if not organic (organics just need to be scrubbed)

leek 1 large, chopped coarsely

celery 2 large sticks, chopped

cloves 6

allspice 1 teaspoon

bay leaves 5

peppercorns 10

water 2 litres or 68fl oz

salt about ⅓ teaspoon

1 Put all the ingredients into a large saucepan.

2 Bring to the boil and simmer slowly for about 4 hours, skimming regularly with a slotted spoon to remove the fat.

3 Strain through a kitchen muslin or sieve.

4 Leave, covered, until completely cold.

5 Skim off any solidified fat.

chicken stock

chicken 1 carcass. Your butcher may sell them after he or she has cut off the legs, drumsticks and breasts for other customers. Otherwise, do it yourself.

water 2 litres or 68fl oz

spring onions 6, leave the green tips on

leek 1 large, trimmed, cleaned and coarsely chopped

celery 2 large stalks, chopped

rosemary 1 large sprig

parsley half a large bunch

sage 1 large sprig

thyme 2 large sprigs

bay leaves 3

white peppercorns 10

salt about 1/3 teaspoon

1 Put the chicken carcass in a large saucepan.

2 Cover with the water.

3 Bring to the boil and simmer for about 60 minutes.

4 Add the rest of the ingredients.

5 Bring back to the boil and simmer for 45 minutes.

6 Strain through a kitchen muslin or sieve.

veal stock

veal bones about 2kg or 4½lb, sawn into 4cm or 1½in lengths, rinsed

onion 1, roughly chopped

carrots 2, trimmed, peeled if not organic (organics just need to be scrubbed), and chopped

celery 2 sticks, chopped

fennel 1 head, chopped

bay leaves 3

thyme 4 large sprigs

peppercorns 10

water 1 litre or 34fl oz

1 Put all the ingredients into a saucepan.

2 Cover with the water.

3 Bring to a boil and simmer for 2 hours, skimming as needed.

4 Strain through a kitchen muslin or sieve.

To make brown veal stock

1 Use the same procedure as above, except first brown the bones in a 200°C or 400°F or gas mark 6 oven for 30 minutes. Spread the bones with tomato purée and brown for another 30 minutes. Drain off the fat, deglaze with some of the water and add to the stockpot with the remaining water.

2 Bring slowly to a boil, then reduce the heat to a simmer. Brown the vegetables in the remaining fat for 5–10 minutes, add 2 tablespoons of tomato paste and then add to the simmering bones with the bay leaves, peppercorns and thyme. Simmer for 2–3 hours. Strain through a kitchen muslin or sieve.

garnishes

meatballs

As well as being a substantial addition to soups, these meatballs are perfect for buffets and picnics.

rapeseed oil 3 tablespoons
spring onions 3, very finely sliced
mince 350g or 12oz, very lean – if it's not lean, dry-fry it first and pour off the fat
herbes de provence 1 teaspoon
egg 1
flour about 4 tablespoons

1 Heat the oil in a large saucepan and gently sauté the spring onions until soft and golden. Leave to cool slightly.

2 Mix the mince with the herbs.

3 Whisk the egg and add to the meat mixture.

4 Using a slotted spoon, lift in the onions and mix well.

5 Form the mixture into small balls – about the size of the top of your thumb.

6 Roll in the flour.

7 Put the meatballs back into the pan – in batches if necessary – and fry until golden.

fish balls

Following the recipe for meatballs, use the same amount of a firm white fish instead of the mince. Again, fish balls are a good addition to buffets and picnics.

simple pastry rounds

puff pastry 1 pack, ready-made
olive oil for brushing

1 Defrost the pastry if necessary.

2 Set the oven to 180°C or 350°F or gas mark 4.

3 Using a small pastry cutter or the top of an appropriately sized bottle or jam pot, etc, cut the pastry into circles about half the size of your soup bowls.

4 Grease a baking tray with olive oil. Arrange the pastry circles on the tray.

5 Brush with more olive oil and bake until golden – about 15 minutes.

cinnamon toast

For sweet soups

demerara sugar 1 tablespoon

cinnamon ½ teaspoon, ground

bread 4 slices wholemeal, cut into rounds with a pastry cutter

redcurrant jelly about 4 tablespoons

1 Mix together the sugar and cinnamon.

2 Set the oven to 180°C or 350°F or gas mark 4.

3 Brush both sides of the bread with redcurrant jelly and dip into the cinnamon mixture.

4 Put onto a baking sheet and bake for 10 minutes each side.

cheese croûtons

olive oil 2 tablespoons

bread 4 slices organic wholemeal, stale

emmental cheese 125g or 4½oz

1 Heat the oil until slightly smoking.

2 Cut the crust off the bread and cut into 1cm or ½in cubes.

3 Grate the cheese finely.

4 Roll the bread in the cheese, pressing it in firmly.

5 Fry in the oil, turning continuously until golden.

herb croûtons

breadcrumbs about 80g or 3oz

fresh soft herbs (mint, parsley, sorrel, coriander, basil, but not tough herbs like rosemary) 2 teaspoons, finely chopped

egg 1 small, whisked

olive oil 3 tablespoons

1 Mix the breadcrumbs with the herbs.

2 Form into small balls about the size of an acorn, then flatten with your hands.

3 Dip into the egg and drain.

4 Heat the oil until smoking slightly.

5 Fry the bread balls until slightly golden – about 2 minutes.

rouille

red pepper 1, halved, peeled and deseeded

tomatoes 100g or 3½oz, canned, drained of most (but not all) of the liquid

garlic 3 cloves, skinned

bread 2 thick slices organic wholemeal, soaked in water

turmeric 1 teaspoon

olive oil 75ml or 3½fl oz, extra-virgin

1 Whiz the peppers, tomatoes and garlic in a food processor.

2 Add the bread and process again.

3 Whisk the turmeric into the olive oil.

4 Pour the olive oil mixture gradually into the food processor, using the pulse to emulsify.

floaters

This is the basic recipe for the most wonderful additions to many of the soups in this book. Add the herbs as instructed or make up ideas of your own, but any herbs you add must be soft herbs, such as parsley, sage, mint, tarragon – not woody herbs like rosemary.

egg 1
flour 150g or 5½oz, wholemeal
black pepper 2 turns of a fresh pepper mill
olive oil 6 tablespoons

1 Whisk the egg, beat in the flour and add the pepper.

2 Grate the vegetables listed below, and squeeze out as much water as possible.

3 Squash them into walnut-sized balls, then flatten them until they're about 1cm or ½in thick and coat them in the batter mixture.

4 Heat the oil and gently sauté them for 3 minutes on each side.

onion floaters
Use 1 very finely grated onion, or 3 large grated spring onions, with 2 teaspoons of chopped fresh oregano.

beetroot floaters
Use 100g or 3½oz of freshly grated raw beetroot mixed with 1 teaspoon of horseradish.

potato floaters
Use about 100g or 3½oz of baking potatoes and be particularly careful to rinse them after they're grated to get rid of the starch. Add 3 teaspoons of fresh, chopped thyme.

courgette floaters
Use about 200g or 7oz of courgettes, trimmed but not peeled. Add 3 tablespoons of chopped flat-leaf parsley.

matzo dumplings

butter 100g or 3½oz, unsalted
eggs 2, beaten
parsley and mint 4 teaspoons, chopped and mixed
matzo meal 90g or or 3¼oz
warm water about 4 tablespoons

1 Mix all the ingredients thoroughly.

2 Leave in the fridge for about 2 hours.

3 Roll the mix into 8 balls – and don't worry if they're very moist.

4 Drop them into the soup.

5 Bring back to a simmer.

6 Leave them to cook for about 15 minutes.

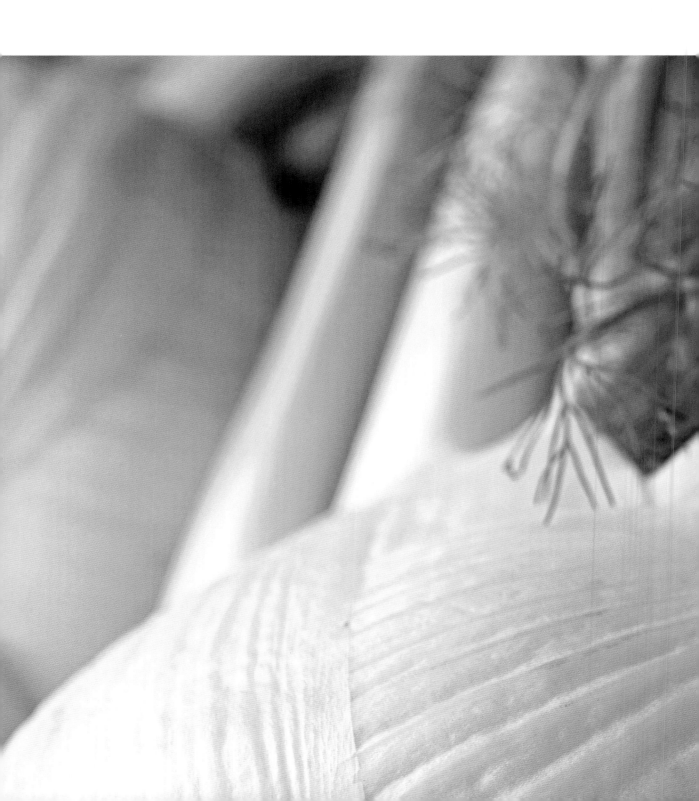

detox and healing

the step-by-step super soup detox plan

Most people wash, bathe or shower every day but how often do you think about cleansing the inside? Apart from the gradual accumulation of environmental toxic chemicals we absorb through breathing, our skin and our food and drink, our bodies also produce their own waste. Much of this is naturally eliminated through the bowels, in the urine, with sweat and your exhaled breath. But much remains as unwanted chemical by-products and damaging free radicals.

As a naturopath, I strongly advise the use of simple 24-hour juice and water fasts as a regular way of maintaining good health. Some of the fittest people I've known in my career have used this simple but ancient therapy.

If regular short fasting does not appeal to you, then an occasional 48-hour regime is an extremely effective body cleanser. These two days can also be completed on water and juices, though by the end of the second day a certain amount of light-headedness may occur, so it's probably advisable not to undertake strenuous physical activity, driving or the use of dangerous machinery. It's sensible to repeat this process once every month or two, and to include some of the soup recipes from this book.

If you need to fast for therapeutic reasons in order to help your body recover from illness, then a three-day period of abstinence is ideal. This is done with a combination of water, juices, good soups and some fresh fruit and vegetables. This fast is certainly not suitable while you're working and should be fitted in when you can have at least one day to recover before going back to your normal activities. For example, you could start on Friday while you are at work, complete the fast on Saturday and Sunday, then have Monday as a day off.

In all fasts, it's usually best to avoid dairy products and animal protein of any kind. To make sure that the ingredients you use are as pure and simple as possible, this really is a time when buying organic produce is extremely important. The best nutritional value of all comes from your own home-made freshly prepared juices, so it's worth investing in a reasonably good juicer.

Fasting produces some side effects, the most common of which is headache, and this occurs even on a 24-hour programme. The drop in blood-sugar levels and the beginnings of elimination are among the triggers, but for many people they're caused by the body being deprived of caffeine. The more coffee you drink, the worse the headache is likely to be, but don't resort to painkillers; simply drink lots more water and it will pass. On two- or three-day fasts, you may start to get what naturopaths call a 'healing crisis', traditionally believed to be caused by the sudden release of accumulated toxins. We now know that it's the result of the natural bacteria in the gut dying off and releasing chemicals that are then absorbed by the gut wall. Increased temperature, sweating, tremors and general aches and pains may happen, but they're a good sign.

Fasting has many health benefits, including an increase in the white-cell count of your blood, which boosts natural immunity. But you do need to exercise caution, especially if you have an underlying illness such as diabetes or you are on prescribed medication that needs to be taken with food: nonsteroidal anti-inflammatories, for example. Fasting can trigger attacks if you suffer from migraine, and although short detox periods are fine during pregnancy and breast feeding, you should not do more than three days. If there are any health problems, always consult your regular physician before starting a detox programme.

24-hour detox for energy

This is the perfect plan for a short, sharp good-health boost that can easily be incorporated into even the most hectic of lifestyles. Though best done on a non-working day, most people in reasonably good health can manage these 24 hours even while working. If you've had a week of entertaining clients, business lunches and overindulgence, a couple of great parties or a bit too much alcohol, these 24 hours will flush the system and revitalize mind and body.

Even without self-inflicted body damage, this simple regime is an excellent way of compensating for the unavoidable environmental hazards to which we're constantly exposed. Used on a regular basis, a 24-hour detox is a huge investment in your good health.

on waking A large glass of hot water with a thick slice of organic unwaxed lemon.

breakfast A large glass of hot water with a thick slice of organic unwaxed lemon. A mug of ginger tea.

mid-morning Another large glass of hot water with a thick slice of organic unwaxed lemon.

lunch A large glass of tomato juice with 2 sticks of celery and a handful of celery leaves whizzed in a liquidizer. Ginger tea.

mid-afternoon Another large glass of hot water with a thick slice of organic unwaxed lemon.

supper Kiwi and pineapple juice: 3 kiwi fruit and enough pineapple to make a large glass. If you haven't got a juicer, look for unsweetened kiwi and pineapple juice and mix together. Ginger tea.

evening Orange juice and almond blend: large glass of orange juice, a tablespoon of flaked almonds, liquidized together.

bedtime Camomile tea with a teaspoon of organic honey.

General Instructions

First thing in the morning make up a jug of parsley tea – a large handful of fresh chopped parsley to 850ml or 1½ pints of boiling water, cover, leave for 10 minutes and strain off the parsley. Keep it in the fridge and drink small glasses regularly throughout the day. This gentle diuretic will help to speed up the detoxifying and cleansing processes, so make sure you drink it all.

You can drink as much water, herb or weak China tea as you like throughout the fast day, but do not add milk or any form of sweetening. You must not consume fizzy water, canned drinks, squashes, cordials, alcohol, Indian tea, coffee or any sweetened drinks. This includes sugar-free commercial products, which contain artificial sweeteners.

48-hour brain-boost detox

Start by following the 24-hour plan, then follow the steps below for day 2.

on waking A large glass of hot water with a thick slice of organic unwaxed lemon.

breakfast A large glass of hot water with a thick slice of organic unwaxed lemon. An orange. Half a pink grapefruit. A slice of cantaloupe. A cup of camomile tea.

mid-morning A large glass of hot water with a thick slice of organic unwaxed lemon.

lunch A large plate of mixed raw red and yellow pepper, cucumber, carrot, radishes, tomatoes, celery and broccoli, with a handful of chopped fresh parsley, a drizzle of extra-virgin olive oil and lemon juice. A large glass of apple juice. A cup of mint tea.

mid-afternoon A mug full of warming, resistance-boosting Mushroom Immunity soup (*see* page 15).

supper A large bowl of fresh fruit salad – any fruit you like, but it must include apple, pear, grapes, mango and some berries, but no banana. One handful of raisins (chew them very slowly) and a handful of fresh unsalted cashew nuts. A glass of unsalted mixed vegetable juice.

evening A large glass of hot water with a thick slice of organic unwaxed lemon.

bedtime Another mug of Mushroom Immunity. A cup of camomile tea with a teaspoon of organic honey.

three-day cleansing detox

A three-day detox is quite a serious undertaking. Though not, strictly speaking, a fast, other than on day one, the limited food intake will produce noticeable side effects and this is definitely best done when you are not working. Because of the very low calorie intake, you will certainly feel quite light-headed by the end of day two and even more so during day three. The severe headaches from day one should have stopped and you may begin to feel euphoric towards the end of this plan.

Because this is a cleansing regime, it's likely that as your body steps up its eliminating processes you may develop unpleasant breath and a coated tongue and pass urine more frequently than normal. It's essential that you keep your fluid intake up to the recommended level to replace lost fluids and to stimulate more elimination. It's unlikely that you will have any unusual problems with wind, but even though you're eating much less bulk than normal, you may find that your bowels may be more active than usual, especially in the latter part of day three.

Take care when you return to normal eating after this three-day plan. It's advisable not to overload your digestive system, so eat little and often, avoid all animal protein, all high-fat and fried foods, and avoid all dairy products, apart from yogurt.

You will need to drink at least 1.5 litres or 54fl oz of fluid on day four. You can eat any fruit and vegetables and introduce some starchy food in the form of oats, wholemeal bread, rice and pasta. A small amount of grilled, poached or steamed white fish would be fine, but don't have shellfish, seafood or oily fish. Do include some resistance- and energy-boosting soups during the days after any period of detox.

Start with the 48-hour brain-boost detox for days one and two. Then, follow the steps on the next page for day three.

on waking A large glass of hot water with a thick slice of organic unwaxed lemon.

breakfast A large glass of hot water with a thick slice of organic unwaxed lemon. A carton of organic low-fat live yogurt with 1 teaspoon of honey, a dessertspoon of raisins and a dessertspoon of chopped hazelnuts. One glass of half-orange, half-grapefruit juice.

mid-morning A mug of Pepper Power soup (*see* page 59). Four dried apricots, 4 prunes.

lunch A large glass of hot water with a thick slice of organic unwaxed lemon. Carrot and red cabbage salad. A cup of mint tea.

mid-afternoon Any unsweetened fruit juice.

supper A mixture of chopped steamed leeks, cabbage, spinach and kale, drizzled with olive oil, lemon juice and a generous sprinkling of nutmeg. Unsweetened red-grape juice. Cup of lime-blossom tea.

evening Another mug of Pepper Power. Four prunes, 4 dates and a small bunch of black grapes.

bedtime A cup of China tea with 2 rice crackers.

supporting and cleansing supplements for super soup detox

No matter whether you choose to do a 24-hour cleansing detox, the 48-hour or three-day programme, you can improve the efficiency of your detox and support your body's whole system by using the appropriate supplements.

general wellbeing

During all these programmes you will be consuming far less food than normal, and even though the recommended foods are those that provide an abundance of nutrients, it is important to give the body an extra supportive boost of vitamins and minerals to avoid possible deficiencies and to guarantee optimum levels of these vital substances. For this reason, you should take the following.

• One high-potency multivitamin and mineral supplement (choose one from a reputable brand leader).

• 500mg vitamin C, three times a day. If you can find it, use ester-C, which many leading manufacturers are now including in their products as this is non-acidic and less likely to cause digestive upsets while you're eating less food.

• A one-a-day standardized extract of cynarin, an extract from globe artichokes. Many toxic substances are fat-soluble and stored in the liver. Cynarin stimulates liver function and helps the body to eliminate these chemicals.

Maintaining proper and regular bowel function is always important, but it is especially so when you are detoxing. On all these regimes there is a much lower fibre intake, which can make the bowels sluggish, so it is more difficult for the normal contractions of your colon to perform their proper function. It's a great advantage to stimulate and maintain bowel function, so you should start to take appropriate measures the day before you begin any of the detox plans.

• To stimulate, improve and maintain bowel function, use 1–2 tablespoons of oat bran or ground psyllium seed. Both provide water-soluble fibre which is better described as 'smoothage' rather than roughage. Do this every night while you follow the plans.

If your immune system has obviously been under par and you've been catching every bug that does the rounds, then you need some additional supportive help. Just by detoxing, you'll be doing your body a favour and helping to boost your natural immunity, but there are additional supplements which you could have.

• Vitamin C and zinc are vital for good immunity and are best taken together in a suckable lozenge.

• Echinacea is one of the most effective herbs for short-term immunity boosting.

• Probiotic (beneficial) bacteria are a key factor in your body's defence mechanism, so get an extra helping of these good bugs by taking a reliable probiotic supplement.

• Guarana provides a gentle energy boost.

• St John's Wort is good if you start to feel a bit low or depressed.

• Ginkgo biloba can help if concentration or short-term memory become a problem during the regime.

general advice

It's important to get plenty of rest while you're detoxing, but what you mustn't do is become a couch potato. Staying in bed a little longer in the morning, having two or three catnaps during the day and going to bed a bit earlier in the evening are all sensible ideas. However, your body also needs some physical activity to stimulate metabolism, energy, hormones, blood flow and digestive function. Take two or three short walks, not more than 10–15 minutes each day, whatever the weather; just make sure you dress appropriately. Do not jog, run, go to the gym, dig the garden, spring-clean the house or get involved in strenuous DIY jobs, as over-exertion will drain your energy, produce a lot of toxic chemical by-products and inhibit your cleansing regime.

detoxing for health

What you've achieved

If you've carefully followed the one-, two- or three-day detoxing programmes, you will have achieved a great deal, as shown below.

• You've helped your body to eliminate a lot of toxic residues.

• You've cleansed your urinary system with a massive increase of fluid throughout, thereby reducing your chances of urinary infection.

• You've rested your liver by drastically reducing the amount of fat in your diet and avoiding the enormous number of chemical flavourings, colourings, preservatives and additives used in the vast majority of commercially prepared foods.

• You've given your entire digestive system a healthy holiday with a minimum amount of animal protein and greatly increased consumption of fruit and vegetables. You will certainly have shortened the transit time of food through your digestive system. Short transit times are a major factor in reducing the risk of inflammatory bowel disease and bowel cancer.

how do you feel?

• You will feel satisfied and pleased with yourself for completing quite a difficult task. The good news is that it will be much easier next time.

• You will feel lighter in spirit as detoxing sharpens the mind and improves focus and concentration. It's not a coincidence that both ancient and modern mystics and religious teachers used fasting as a way of increasing their spiritual awareness and their ability to focus on solving great problems.

• You will feel lighter in body as you will certainly have lost some weight if you needed to, but this lightness is not just because you're carrying a smaller physical load; it's because your whole metabolic process will be running at its most efficient and firing on all cylinders.

• You will feel more energetic because your metabolism expends less energy on wasteful tasks like dealing with junk food and excessive alcohol and is able to concentrate solely on converting the healthy ingredients that you are consuming into easily available energy.

foods that heal

Naturopaths have always believed that food could heal, and for at least 7,000 years medicine men, wise women, healers and ancient practitioners have used the power of many different foods. Now, in the 21st century, there is a growing body of science that supports these ancient theories – so much so that many leading research organizations advise dietary changes as a way to prevent and treat disease.

In the following pages you will find a very simple guide to using your own kitchen as nature's pharmacy. No prescriptions, no visits to the doctor, no waiting at the chemist; just a wide range of delicious foods that you can incorporate into a huge selection of recipes for making wonderful and beneficial soups and other dishes. All fruits, vegetables, nuts, seeds, meat, fish and poultry contain a host of natural chemicals that make up the nutritional value of everything you eat, and these nutrients are essential for good health.

In addition, certain plant chemicals have specific therapeutic benefits. The pink mouthwash at the dentist's, for example, contains a strong antiseptic called thymol. This substance occurs naturally in the herb thyme, which is where it was first discovered. Equally surprising is the fact that Ancient Greeks used extracts of wild lettuce as a sleeping potion. When you cut a lettuce stalk, a sticky white substance comes out that contains powerfully hypnotic, morphine-like chemicals. All modern lettuces are descended from the original wild variety and contain tiny amounts of the same chemical, so a bowl of Spiced Lettuce Soup (*see* page 69) is just what you need if sleep is a problem. Arthritis, rheumatism or gout? Then try Chill-out Treat (*see* page 14), as it is made with apples. The special soluble fibre they contain, known as pectin, not only helps lower cholesterol and blood pressure, but also helps alleviate the pain and discomfort of joint problems. Plus, the vitamin C and antioxidants from the currants help protect against some forms of cancer.

In these pages you'll find help for acne and anaemia, cholesterol and coughs, gallstones and gingivitis, heartburn and herpes, menstrual problems and mouth ulcers, even varicose veins. Of course, soup won't cure serious health problems, but it will certainly help. If you're taking prescribed medication and add the appropriate foods to your daily diet, it will also speed your recovery.

condition	ingredients	effect
Acne	Dandelion Fennel Garlic	Cleansing and diuretic. Stimulates liver and improves fat digestion. Antibacterial.
Anaemia	Chicory, Watercress, Dates, Poultry	All are good sources of iron.
Anxiety	Basil Rosemary Buckwheat	Contains mood-enhancing linalool. A traditional brain-booster. Improves blood flow to the brain.
Arthritis	Apples Cabbage Celery Mussels Turnip Dandelion leaves	For anti-inflammatory pectin and malic acid. Contains healing mucilage. Stimulates excretion of uric acid. Contain anti-inflammatory oils. Eliminates uric acid. Diuretic and cleansing.
Asthma	Garlic Carrots Onions Lemon juice	Reduces mucus. Contain lung-healing betacarotene. Rich in antibacterial sulphur compounds. For protective vitamin C and bioflavonoids.
Back pain	Thyme Radishes Walnuts	For muscle-relaxing volatile oils. Contain pain-relieving mustard oils. Rich in anti-inflammatory oils.
Bronchitis	Onion, Garlic, Chives Coriander Asparagus, Parsley	For antibacterial sulphur compounds. Contains coriandrol, a natural decongestant. Gentle diuretics to relieve congestion.
Catarrh	Garlic Leeks Parsley	For antibacterial sulphur compounds. An effective decongestant. For its diuretic properties.
Chilblains	Basil, Chives, Coriander, Chilli	All contain vitamins and phytochemicals that help stimulate circulation.
Cholesterol	Garlic Chives Olive oil Beans	For the phytochemical allicin, which eliminates cholesterol. Lower cholesterol, like all members of the onion family. For mono-unsaturated fats that reduce cholesterol. For soluble fibre that lowers cholesterol.
Chronic fatigue	Basil Almonds Beetroot Chicory	Contains mood-enhancing volatile oils. A rich source of energy, protein, B vitamins and zinc. As a blood-builder, cleanser and tonic. Another powerful tonic, cleanser and detoxifier.

condition	ingredients	effect
Circulation problems	Chives	Like all members of the onion family, stimulate the circulation.
	Coriander	Improves peripheral circulation.
	Cabbage	A rich source of mustard oils, which help speed blood flow.
	Buckwheat	Contains rutin, which strengthens blood vessels.
	Mackerel	Provides essential fatty acids – essential for healthy circulation.
Cold	Garlic	A rich source of antibacterial and antiviral sulphur compounds.
	Thyme	Contains thymol, a powerful antiseptic.
	Blueberries	A powerful protective package of antioxidants.
	Oranges	Rich in protective vitamin C.
	Kiwi	Rich in vitamin C, as well as vitamin E and betacarotene.
Constipation	Dandelion leaves	Supply phytochemicals that stimulate the colon.
	Root vegetables	Rich in fibre to promote regularity.
	Dried beans	Contain soluble fibre, which improves bowel function.
	Live yogurt	Contains beneficial bacteria for good digestion.
	Raisins	Like all dried fruits, are rich in soluble fibre.
Cough	Garlic	An antibacterial.
	Thyme	An antibacterial and expectorant.
	Turnips	Contain the sulphur compound raphanol, a bactericide.
	Watercress	Contains benzyl oils, which are antibacterial, and other phytochemicals that protect lung tissue.
Cystitis	Parsley	A gentle diuretic, which maintains a good flow of urine.
	Pumpkin seeds	A rich source of zinc – important for the urinary system.
	Sage	Contains volatile oils that are a urinary antiseptic.
	Asparagus	Provides the kidney stimulant asparagines; use the cooking water in soups and sauces.
Depression	Basil	Helps the anxiety that often accompanies depression.
	Buckwheat	Contains rutin, which helps lift depression and promote energy.
	Apples	A rich package of nutrients with physical and mental tonic effects.
	Leeks	Rich in potassium and powerfully cleansing for mind and body.
Diarrhoea	Mint	An effective antacid, which helps settle the stomach.
	Garlic	For diarrhoea caused by food poisoning.
	Apples	Contain malic acid, which soothes the stomach lining.
	Rice	A traditional Eastern treatment for diarrhoea.
Diverticulitis	Sage	Astringent and cleansing to the gut.
	Mint	An effective antacid and helps settle the stomach.
	Live yogurt	Provides beneficial bacteria for better digestion.
	Lentils	For essential bulk and soluble fibre.
Flatulence	Fennel	Contains fenchone, which relieves wind – and colic in children.
	Mint	A traditional digestive aid to relieve flatulence.
	Caraway seeds	The phytochemicals prevent flatulence when added to cabbage and bean dishes.

condition	ingredients	effect
Fluid retention	Parsley, Dandelion leaves, Celery	All are effective natural diuretics.
Gallstones	Artichokes	Contain natural chemicals that stimulate the gall bladder.
	Tarragon	Contains volatile oils that improve liver function.
	Pineapple	Provides the healing enzyme bromelain to counteract any inflammation.
Gingivitis	Lemon	Super-rich in vitamin C for healthy gums.
	Sage	Cleansing and strongly antibacterial.
	Thyme	Provides the antiseptic chemical thymol.
	Apples	Massage the gums and promote healing.
Gout	Dandelion tea	A diuretic that helps remove uric acid.
	Olive oil	A rich source of mono-unsaturated fats, which ease joint pain.
	Strawberries	Contrary to popular belief, are not bad for gout but also reduce uric acid levels and relieve pain.
	Dark-green cabbage	Contains anti-arthritic properties.
Hair problems	Prawns	Like all shellfish, very rich in zinc; essential for healthy hair.
	Pumpkin seeds	One of the best plant sources of zinc.
	Avocado	An excellent source of vitamin E.
	Horseradish	Helps improve circulation to the scalp.
Halitosis	Anise, Dill, Fennel seeds, Parsley	Can all be chewed to freshen the breath.
	Celery	Contains fibrous tissue to massage the gums and protect against gingivitis, a common cause of breath problems.
Headache	Sage	Contains plant hormones that help regulate the menstrual cycle and relieve headaches associated with PMS.
	Dandelion leaves	Diuretic, for headaches caused by fluid retention.
	Artichokes	A liver cleanser for headaches caused by overindulgence.
Heartburn	Mint	The most effective remedy of all. A glass of mint tea sweetened with a little honey after each meal and at bedtime will help relieve heartburn almost instantly.
Heart disease	Garlic	Lowers blood pressure and cholesterol, as well as reducing the stickiness of the blood. Eat at least one whole clove daily in food.
	Parsley	Protects against high blood pressure through its diuretic activities.
	All the berries	Antioxidant and heart-protective, so use regularly.
	Apples	Two a day can help to lower cholesterol levels.
	Beans	Provide soluble fibre, which lowers cholesterol.
	Oatmeal	Contains soluble fibre and vitamin E for a healthy heart.
	Whitebait	Like all oily fish, contains heart-protective fatty acids, but no damaging saturated fats.

condition	ingredients	effect
Hepatitis	Globe artichokes	Stimulate the function of the gall bladder and improve liver function.
	Chicory	Contains bitter natural substances that stimulate liver and digestion.
	Tarragon	Exerts beneficial effects on the liver and gall bladder and should be added to food.
Herpes	Lemon balm	Specifically antiviral and a great aid in the treatment of all forms of herpes. Add it to any salad.
	Garlic	A strong antiviral agent; eat at least one whole clove of garlic a day.
Hypertension	Garlic	Lowers blood pressure and cholesterol, as well as reducing the stickiness of the blood. Eat at least one whole clove daily in food.
	Parsley	A good diuretic that helps eliminate excessive fluid and thus lowers blood pressure.
	Tomatoes	Rich in lycopene, an antioxidant that protects the heart and blood vessels.
	Lentils	Contain a special type of fibre that helps to control blood pressure.
	Tofu	Rich in plant hormones that help to lower blood pressure.
Indigestion	Mint	The most effective remedy of all. A glass of mint tea sweetened with a little honey after each meal and at bedtime will help relieve indigestion almost instantly.
	Fennel	Anise is an excellent remedy for indigestion.
	Apples	Rich in malic acid, an effective antacid.
Influenza	Blueberries	Lots of vitamin C and antioxidants.
	Watercress	Rich in mustard oils, which are antiviral, and phytochemicals, which protect lung tissue.
	Carrots	Contain huge amounts of betacarotene – vital for a healthy immune system.
	Yogurt	Provides beneficial bacteria that stimulate immunity.
Insomnia	Lettuce	All varieties contain tiny amounts of morphine-like chemicals to help you sleep.
	Chickpeas	Contain calcium and tryptophan, both sleep-inducers.
	Basil	Supplies volatile oils that are calming and relaxing.
	Rice and potato	Are good sources of sleep-inducing tryptophan.
Laryngitis	Sage	Especially good for all throat problems, as it contains the antibacterial volatile oil thujone. Add to salads and use as a tea for gargling.
	Pineapple	A rich source of the enzyme bromelain, which is specifically effective in the relief of sore throats.
	Leeks	A traditional remedy for throat and voice problems, as they contain many antibacterial natural chemicals.

condition	ingredients	effect
Menstrual problems	Tofu, Beans, Sage	Rich in natural isoflavones, which help regulate hormone levels.
	Dates	Provide iron to combat anaemia.
	Olive oil	A good source of vitamin E, which helps reduce menstrual discomfort.
	Pumpkin seeds	Supply zinc and vitamin E, which both help with menstrual problems.
	Wholemeal bread	For B vitamins, including B_6, which are all important for normal menstruation.
Mouth ulcers	Garlic	Eating plenty of garlic helps, but the best treatment is to rub the ulcers with the cut squeezed end of a clove of garlic. Though this may be quite uncomfortable at the time, it will heal them quickly.
	Thyme	The best source of the natural healing antiseptic oil thymol.
Obesity	Soups made with all vegetables, pasta, rice and potatoes	Excellent as part of a weight-loss regime. They're filling, nourishing, sustaining and, mostly, low-fat.
Raynaud's Syndrome	Basil, Chives, Coriander	All contain vitamins and phytochemicals tht help stimulate circulation. Add to as many salads as possible.
	Horseradish	A powerful circulatory stimulant.
	Chillies	Provide the powerful circulatory stimulant capsaicin.
	Ginger	Contains the essential oil gingerol, which stimulates blood flow to the tiniest blood vessels in the hands and feet.
Restless legs	Chicken, Turkey	For iron to prevent anaemia, a common cause of restless legs.
	Tomatoes	Provide potassium to prevent cramp.
	Herrings	Rich in essential fatty acids, which improve circulation.
	Onions	Help reduce cholesterol and improve blood flow.
SAD (Seasonal Affective Disorder)	Basil	Helps the anxiety that often accompanies SAD; add to salads and sandwiches.
	Bread, Potatoes, Rice, Oats, Pasta	All good sources of complex carbohydrates, which help maintain even blood-sugar levels and reduce the ups and downs of SAD.
	Shellfish	A rich source of zinc, essential to fight the chronic fatigue that goes with SAD.
Sinusitis	Horseradish	Contains volatile oils that help clear the sinuses.
	Chillies	Rich in capsaicin, which stimulates the lining of the sinuses and clears the mucus.
	Papaya	Contains healing enzymes that benefit all mucous membranes.
	Cabbage	Rich in antibacterial sulphur compounds that fight infection.
	Strawberries	A rich source of immunity-boosting vitamin C.
Varicose veins	Basil, Chives, Coriander	All contain vitamins and phytochemicals that help stimulate circulation. Use generously in salads.
	Chillies	Are a rich source of capsaicin, which stimulates and improves circulation.
	All nuts and seeds	Contain vitamin E, which is important for the health of blood vessels.

index

Grateful acknowledgement is made for permission to reprint from the
following previously published work: extract on page 6 from *Miss Manner's
Guide to Excruciatingly Correct Behaviour* by Judith Martin (W W Norton,
1995). The author and publisher apologise for any errors or omissions and
would be grateful to be notified of any corrections that should be
incorporated in a reprint.